I.M. PEI

ASIAN AMERICANS OF ACHIEVEMENT

Margaret Cho

Daniel Inouye

Maxine Hong Kingston

Michelle Kwan

Ang Lee

Bruce Lee

Maya Lin

Yo-Yo Ma

Isamu Noguchi

Apolo Anton Ohno

I.M. Pei

Anna Sui

Amy Tan

Vera Wang

Kristi Yamaguchi

Jerry Yang

ASIAN AMERICANS
OF ACHIEVEMENT

I.M. PEI

LOUISE CHIPLEY SLAVICEK

CHELSEA HOUSE
PUBLISHERS
An imprint of Infobase Publishing

I.M. Pei

Chelsea House
An imprint of Infobase Publishing
132 West 31st Street
New York, NY 10001

Library of Congress Cataloging-in-Publication Data
Slavicek, Louise Chipley, 1956-
  I.M. Pei / Louise Chipley Slavicek.
    p. cm. — (Asian Americans of achievement)
  Includes bibliographical references and index.
  ISBN 978-1-60413-567-1 (hardcover)
  1. Pei, I. M., 1917- 2. Chinese American architects—Biography—Juvenile literature.
  3. Architects—United States—Biography—Juvenile literature. I. Pei, I. M., 1917-
  II. Title. III. Series.
  NA737.P365S53 2009
  720.92—dc22
  [B]   2009014609

Chelsea House books are available at special discounts when purchased in
bulk quantities for businesses, associations, institutions, or sales promotions.
Please call our Special Sales Department in New York at (212) 967-8800
or (800) 322-8755.

You can find Chelsea House on the World Wide Web at http://www.chelseahouse.com

Series design by Erika K. Arroyo
Cover design by Ben Peterson

Printed in the United States of America

Bang EJB 10 9 8 7 6 5 4 3 2 1

This book is printed on acid-free paper.

All links and Web addresses were checked and verified to be correct at the time of
publication. Because of the dynamic nature of the Web, some addresses and links
may have changed since publication and may no longer be valid.

CONTENTS

1

"Pharaoh Pei's Pyramid"

During an extraordinary career that has lasted for seven decades, Chinese-American architect I.M. Pei has designed many well-known buildings throughout the world, from museums and symphony halls to high-rise office towers and scientific centers. Yet none of his buildings is as famous—or as controversial—as the glittering glass pyramid he designed for the Louvre museum in Paris. When Pei first revealed his plan for the pyramid to the French people in 1984, a firestorm of protest and anger swept the nation.

PEI'S MOST HATED—AND BELOVED—CREATION

Constructed over a period of eight centuries, the Louvre was a royal fortress and palace before it was converted into one of the world's leading art museums in the late 1700s. Most French people viewed the historic and lavishly decorated building as their nation's supreme architectural and cultural treasure.

The career of Chinese-American architect I.M. Pei, shown here in 1986, has
spanned seven decades. His most prominent projects have included the
East Building of the National Gallery of Art in Washington, D.C., the Bank
of China Tower in Hong Kong, and an expansion of the Louvre museum
in Paris. His plans for the Louvre, however, were initially met with scorn in
France.

Consequently, when President François Mitterrand announced in 1982 that the French government was funding a major expansion of the beloved landmark, they enthusiastically backed the project. Without question, the Louvre needed more space. The palace-turned-museum lacked many essential support facilities, including conservation workshops, storage areas, and such basic guest services as information booths and a cafeteria. Although there was some grumbling at first when Mitterrand chose Pei instead of a French architect to design the expansion, Pei's decision to put the addition underground rather than building onto one of the palace's three wings made a favorable impression on the French public.

Then, in January 1984, Pei dropped a bombshell. He unveiled his blueprint for a 71-foot-tall (22-meter-tall) glass pyramid to be placed right in the middle of the Louvre's central courtyard, above his planned underground extension to the museum. Aside from providing a dramatic entrance to the museum, the glass structure was to serve as a skylight for the big new reception hall below. Pei was convinced that his pyramid design had many advantages as the Louvre's new entryway. One of the most important, he declared, was that the nearly transparent pyramid would divert less attention from the palace's classic architecture than a more traditional rectangular building of brick or stone. Pei's arguments, however, did not persuade a shocked French public and press.

Although Mitterrand loyally backed his hand-chosen architect's unconventional design, public opinion in France was overwhelmingly against what the media called "Pharaoh Pei's pyramid." Without exception, the country's top newspapers denounced the proposed entryway as flashy and undignified. "You rub your eyes. You think you're dreaming; it seems that you've gone back to the era of castles for sale and Hollywood copies of the temple of Solomon, of Alexander, of Cleopatra. . . . It doesn't seem justified to treat the courtyard of the Louvre like a Disneyland annex," sniffed a commentator for the popular French newspaper *Le Monde*. Another leading French paper, *Le Figaro*, published the results of a survey showing that 90 percent of its readership thought Pei's ultra-modern structure would look out of place on the Louvre's stately grounds and should not be built.

Despite the outcry, plans for the pyramid went forward, and in March 1989, Pei's large underground expansion to the Louvre, along with its controversial entryway, opened to the public. When the French people actually saw the jewel-like pyramid firsthand, many had a dramatic change of heart. The nearly universal hostility that had greeted "Pharaoh Pei's pyramid" when the design was first made public five years earlier was replaced by nearly unanimous admiration for the boldly original, high-tech structure. "The much-feared pyramid has become adorable," admitted a commentator in the Parisian newspaper *Le Quotidien de Paris*. Today, 20 years after it was completed, Pei's famous creation has become one of Paris's most beloved icons, rivaling the Eiffel Tower as the city's chief symbol on travel brochures and postcards.

By the time the Louvre pyramid and expansion opened in 1989, Pei had already established himself as one of America's leading architects, with such acclaimed structures as the East Building of the National Gallery of Art in Washington, D.C., and the National Center for Atmospheric Research in Boulder, Colorado. But after his renovation of the Louvre, Pei was generally recognized as one of the most original and influential architects of the entire twentieth century. He would never again take on a project that attracted as much international attention as the Louvre expansion. Nonetheless, during the two decades since his spectacular pyramid made its debut, Pei has designed a number of powerful and critically acclaimed buildings. Among the most outstanding are the technically

Many people in France were outraged when they first learned that I.M. Pei planned to build a glass pyramid in the main courtyard of the Louvre. But after the pyramid opened in 1989 as the new entryway to the museum, Pei's design drew much praise. The Louvre pyramid is now one of Paris's leading landmarks.

brilliant Bank of China Tower in Hong Kong, the exquisite Miho Museum near Kyoto, Japan, and the Museum of Islamic Art in Doha, Qatar, which was completed in 2008 when Pei was 91 years old. In the Museum of Islamic Art, as in many of his other most important buildings, Pei successfully blends the traditional with the modern to create a structure that reflects the culture, history, and spirit of its surroundings while also pointing toward the future. In his acceptance speech for the prestigious Pritzker Architecture Prize in 1983, Pei spoke about his chosen profession and what he considered as its noblest aims, goals he has faithfully tried to fulfill throughout his long architectural career:

> Architects by design investigate the play of volumes in light, explore the mysteries of movement in space, examine the measure that is scale and proportion, and above all, they search for that special quality that is the spirit of the place as no building exists alone. . . . Let us all be attentive to new ideas, to advancing means, to dawning needs, to impetuses of change so that we may achieve, beyond architectural originality, a harmony of spirit in the service of man.

2

Chinese Roots

On April 26, 1917, in southern China's bustling port of Guangzhou, Tsuyee and Lien Kwun Pei proudly welcomed their second child and first son into the world. They named the baby Ieoh Ming, meaning "to inscribe brightly." According to Chinese astrology, 1917 was the "Year of the Snake." People born under the sign of the Snake are supposed to be charming, intelligent, and creative. They are also said to be unusually determined and independent-minded.

FROM GUANGZHOU TO HONG KONG

Ieoh Ming's parents both grew up in east-central China, in the picturesque and ancient town of Suzhou, where their families had lived for many generations. But Tsuyee's successful career with the Bank of China had taken the couple far from their quiet and stately hometown to major cities in central and northern China, including the national capital, Beijing. In 1914, Tsuyee's employer sent him southward to Guangzhou, where Ieoh Ming and his older sister, Yuen Hua, were born. Before Ieoh Ming had turned two, Tsuyee was transferred again—this time at his own request—to the British colony of Hong Kong.

Tsuyee Pei's desire to leave the Chinese mainland to work and live in Hong Kong was rooted in his growing concerns for the safety of his young family. Ieoh Ming was born during a particularly unsettled time in China's long history. Five years before his birth, in 1912, rebel forces led by Dr. Sun Yat-sen overthrew the Chinese emperor and proclaimed the founding of the Republic of China. But Sun Yat-sen's hopes of uniting his vast homeland under a strong, democratic government were quickly dashed. China soon fell under the sway of a military dictator, General Yuan Shikai, and Sun was forced into exile. In 1916, Yuan died unexpectedly, creating a power vacuum in China. In one province after another, local warlords (military strongmen) fought their way into power. China was plunged into a bloody civil war as Sun Yat-sen and his followers, the Nationalists, battled the warlords for control of the country.

Anxious to get his family out of harm's way, Tsuyee persuaded his superiors at the Bank of China in 1918 to transfer him to the company's Hong Kong office. Hong Kong had been a British colony since the early 1840s, when Great Britain defeated China in the Opium War. As part of the treaty that ended the war, the Chinese emperor was forced to turn over Hong Kong Island, including its excellent deepwater port, to the British. Hong Kong is located only 75 miles (120 kilometers) southeast of Guangzhou. Yet, because the colony was protected by the might of the British imperial army, Tsuyee felt confident that his family would be safe there.

Living in the British colony gave young Ieoh Ming a window on the world outside of China, especially on the West. By the early 1900s, after more than 50 years of British rule, the port of Hong Kong had become a major entrepôt for world trade and one of the most cosmopolitan cities in Asia. In 1918, nearly 600,000 people lived in Hong Kong, including tens of thousands of Europeans—chiefly Britons but also Germans, French, and Portuguese, among other nationalities. In common with many other sons of well-to-do Chinese parents in Hong Kong, when Ieoh Ming was old enough to begin his formal education, he attended a school run by English Protestant missionaries, with classes taught in English and Chinese. Tsuyee himself had attended an American missionary school in Suzhou, and his training in English had been very useful in his banking career. He was convinced that a basic understanding of English and a "modern," Western-style education would be an advantage to Ieoh Ming in whatever career path his son chose to follow.

A NEW HOME IN SHANGHAI

By late 1927, the Nationalists, who were led by General Chiang Kai-shek following the death of Sun Yat-sen two years earlier, had finally managed to drive the warlords from power in most of China. Now that peace had returned to the mainland, Tsuyee happily accepted a promotion as manager of the Bank of China's big office in Shanghai, in east-central China. During his nine years in Hong Kong, Tsuyee had made a name for himself as a foreign exchange expert, and his future with the bank appeared bright. Tsuyee's family, as well as his career, had thrived in the British colony. By the time the Pei family moved to Shanghai in 1927, Ieoh Ming and Yuen Hua had three younger siblings: a sister, Wei, and two brothers, Kwun and Chung.

Located at the mouth of Asia's longest river, the Yangtze, Shanghai was China's busiest international port, main financial and industrial hub, and most densely populated city during the 1920s. It was also even more cosmopolitan and Western-oriented than Hong Kong was. Nicknamed the "Paris of the East," Shanghai was known for its diverse international population, ornate European-style buildings, and lively, sophisticated nightlife. To the embarrassment of most of the city's Chinese

residents, however, Shanghai's greatest claim to fame was its
rampant vice—including gambling, prostitution, and a booming illegal drug trade. "In no city, West or East, have I ever had
such an impression of dense, rank, richly clotted life," the British novelist Aldous Huxley wrote of Shanghai in 1926. "Nothing more intensely living can be imagined."

Shanghai first became a center of Western influence in
China following the Opium War of 1839–1842. As part of the
same humiliating peace treaty that gave Hong Kong to Great
Britain, China's emperor was forced to open Shanghai and
several other Chinese ports to British trade and residence.
Because the port's location at the point where the Yangtze emp-
ties into the East China Sea was ideal for international trade,
the French and U.S. governments pressured the emperor into
giving them commercial rights and "concessions" in Shanghai,
too. In international law, a concession is a tract of land within a
country that is administered by another country's government.
Typically, it is *conceded* or surrendered by a militarily weaker
state to a stronger one. Many of Shanghai's Chinese residents
bitterly resented the fact that the concessions' foreign residents
did not have to obey Chinese laws. Instead, the British, French,
and American citizens who lived in the different concessions
were only obliged to obey the laws of their countries.

Shanghai's Chinese inhabitants were permitted to live and
work in all the foreign concessions. The concessions' wealthier
Chinese residents, including professionals and successful busi-
nessmen like Tsuyee Pei, typically clustered together in small
and exclusive neighborhoods. Soon after moving to Shanghai,
Tsuyee bought a modern, European-style house in an upper-
class Chinese enclave inside the French Concession. In common with most of his well-to-do neighbors, he sent Ieoh Ming
and his two younger brothers to a private, Western-run school
that served the sons of Shanghai's Chinese elite. Ieoh Ming's
new school, St. John's, was operated by American Protestant

missionaries and featured a Western-style curriculum taught almost entirely in English. By the time he graduated from St. John's at age 18, I.M. Pei could read the Bible and the classic novels of British author Charles Dickens in English and speak English reasonably fluently.

SUZHOU

Ieoh Ming's formal schooling in Shanghai was strongly shaped by modern Western culture and ideals. Nonetheless, young I.M. Pei also learned a great deal about the ancient traditions and values of his homeland during his years in Shanghai. Ieoh Ming's chief instructors in China's rich and time-honored culture were his older relatives in the Pei ancestral residence of Suzhou, particularly his grandfather, Li-tai Pei. Before moving to Shanghai, Ieoh Ming had never even met Li-tai. Guangzhou was nearly 1,000 miles (1,600 kilometers) from Suzhou, and Hong Kong was even farther away. Ieoh Ming's home in western Shanghai, however, was just 40 miles (64 kilometers) from Suzhou, so he could easily visit his grandfather on holidays and school breaks. Eager to make up for lost time, Li-tai invited Ieoh Ming to stay with him often, especially during his grandson's long summer vacations.

Whenever Ieoh Ming came to see him in Suzhou, Li-tai made a point of discussing the family finances with him. Since Ieoh Ming was one of his oldest grandsons, Li-tai realized that he could end up in charge of the family's extensive properties someday. After settling in Suzhou during the 1300s, Ieoh Ming's ancestors had made a considerable fortune through selling traditional Chinese medicines. They put most of their profits into buying land, which they then rented to small farmers. Soon, the Pei family had become one of Suzhou's largest and wealthiest landlords.

Making sure that Ieoh Ming understood the family business was very important to Li-tai. Yet, he was even more concerned about instructing his grandson in the ancient wisdom and practices of Confucianism. The cornerstone of traditional Chinese culture and thought, Confucianism is a system of moral principles based on the teachings of the philosopher Confucius, who lived from 551 to 479 B.C. Confucianism focuses on the questions of how to live a truly virtuous life and build a harmonious and stable society. Above all, it emphasizes respect for a fixed hierarchy (power structure) of relationships within the family and society as a whole. For example, according to Confucianism, sons should submit to the authority of

OLD AND NEW: GROWING UP IN SUZHOU AND SHANGHAI

Recently, I.M. Pei talked to an interviewer about what it was like to divide his time between Shanghai, China's most modern and Westernized city during the 1920s and 1930s, and ancient and conservative Suzhou, the Pei family's ancestral residence. He observed:

Shanghai was a city of tremendous vitality. . . . It was very international in character and therefore open-minded and tolerant. The new buildings that went up in Shanghai obviously had an influence on me. I was quite taken, as a matter of a fact, that they were able to build taller and taller buildings. That was very unusual. In Suzhou we had only one-, two-, or three-story buildings and that was all, but in Shanghai they were building 10, 20, and 30 stories. . . . I was exposed to the new in architecture and the arts, but also in lifestyle. It was a very exciting, but also a very corrupt place. So I learned both good and bad from Shanghai. The good part of it was that I saw a little of the future in Shanghai that I was not able to see in Suzhou. In Suzhou I was very much conscious of the past, but in Shanghai I saw the future.

After the Pei family moved to Shanghai in 1927, young I.M. often visited his grandfather in the family's ancestral hometown, Suzhou. There, he wandered through the family's private garden, Shizilin *(above)*, or Forest of Stone Lions, known for its weathered rock sculptures.

their fathers, wives to the authority of their husbands, and subjects to the authority of their rulers. Although Confucianism itself is not a religion, Confucius had enormous respect for China's age-old spiritual traditions. Consequently, he urged his followers to practice the ancient Chinese custom of ancestor worship. Ancestor worship involves the offering of regular sacrificial feasts to dead relatives in special "ancestral halls" or temples. The offerings are made both to honor the deceased relations and to win their favor.

As China modernized and became ever more oriented toward the West during the early twentieth century, the Confucian values that had once underpinned Chinese society began to lose their grip over the Chinese people. This drifting away from the Confucian ideals and practices of China's past, especially among the country's young people, bothered Li-tai a great deal. Therefore, in addition to having Ieoh Ming study the classic Confucian writings, Li-tai often took him to the Pei ancestral hall in the hills near Suzhou, so that his grandson could learn the ceremonies of ancestor worship. Years later, I.M. Pei fondly recalled that, for him, his proud and dignified grandfather "was the very symbol of Confucian values. It seemed to me that his lifestyle was totally untouched by the West."

Some of I.M. Pei's most cherished memories from his childhood visits to Suzhou center on the family's large ornamental garden, Shizilin, or the "Forest of Stone Lions." The city of Suzhou has long been famous throughout China for its exquisite private gardens, many of which, like Shizilin, were first built hundreds of years ago. The artfully designed gardens typically featured miniature waterfalls, winding pathways, graceful pavilions, and tall, unusually shaped rock "sculptures" harvested from a nearby lake. The Forest of Stone Lions got its name from its distinctive weathered rock sculptures, which were said to resemble dancing lions. More than 75 years later, Pei vividly recalled the many happy hours he spent in the Shizilin garden, playing make-believe with his young cousins. "The whole garden was of course an ideal playground for us," he reminisced. "I found that the caves in the rocks, the stone bridges, the ponds and waterfalls were most stimulating to our fantasies."

IEOH MING AND HIS MOTHER

Ieoh Ming suffered a terrible tragedy three years after his family moved from Hong Kong to Shanghai, when he was 13 years old. His beloved mother, Lien Kwun, developed cancer and

BUDDHISM IN CHINA

One of the world's great religions, Buddhism was founded in India in the 500s B.C. by Siddhartha Gautama, or the Buddha ("Enlightened One"), as he came to be known. Buddhism is believed to have first reached China during the early second century A.D. by means of the Silk Road, the famous overland trade routes that connected China with the rest of the Asian continent and the West. After its introduction to China, Buddhism quickly attracted followers from all walks of life, from wealthy landowners to impoverished peasants, and Buddhist monasteries and temples sprang up throughout the country.

The central principle, or "Noble Truth," of Buddhism is that life is suffering—a continuous cycle of birth, illness, aging, and death. To be released from this endlessly repeating "Wheel of Life," people must learn to put aside their worldly ambitions and cravings and follow an "Eightfold Path" of right action, judgment, speech, livelihood, memory, obedience, meditation, and faith. Then their souls could attain Nirvana, a state of complete and eternal peace and enlightenment.

died. Although Ieoh Ming respected his father, he had never felt particularly close to him. Distant and formal in his relations with his children, his father "was not the sort of man to pat a son on the back, or hug a daughter," I.M. Pei later revealed to an interviewer. In contrast, Lien Kwun was unfailingly warm and understanding—"someone I would go to for advice," Pei recalled.

A devout Buddhist, Lien Kwun had often taken Ieoh Ming along on her religious retreats, including one at a serene mountaintop site where it was so quiet he thought he could hear the bamboo growing in a nearby grove. On another occasion, she took Ieoh Ming to a retreat in a Buddhist monastery, where they sat for hours at a time in silent meditation. "This was a great gift that my mother had given me, to hear the silence," Pei said years later. Pei also credits his lifelong appreciation for traditional Chinese music and art to Lien Kwun, who was an accomplished flute player and calligrapher. Considered equal to painting in China, East Asian calligraphy is the art of writing Chinese characters with brush and ink.

After Lien Kwun was diagnosed with cancer, she entrusted her eldest son with the responsibility of preparing and administering the opium her doctors had prescribed to help ease her pain. (Opium is an addictive narcotic drug made from the seedpods of a certain type of poppy plant.) Although he knew all along that his mother was gravely ill, Ieoh Ming was overwhelmed with shock and grief when she finally succumbed to her cancer. Yet, even though he was just 13, I.M. was expected to put aside his own sorrow and be strong for his sisters and brothers. "The last thing she told me was to take care of my brothers and sisters and to set an example," he later recalled. "As the oldest son, I was supposed to understand."

3

Studying in America

By the end of his junior year in high school, 17-year-old Ieoh Ming Pei had begun to think seriously about his future. During the 1920s and 1930s, it was common for the sons of well-to-do Chinese families to attend college abroad, particularly in Europe. Tsuyee Pei wanted Ieoh Ming to apply to Oxford, a highly respected English university. Besides Oxford's outstanding academic reputation, Tsuyee liked the school's location. Tsuyee had made a number of English friends through his international banking connections and felt confident they would help to keep an eye on his son while he was at Oxford. Ieoh Ming, though, had other ideas. He wanted to go to college in the United States.

AMERICA AND CHINA

The curriculum at St. John's was demanding, and Ieoh Ming had to work hard to hold onto his place as one of the top students in his class. When he was not studying, he loved to play billiards with his friends or go to one of Shanghai's three movie

theaters to see the latest Hollywood picture. Ieoh Ming especially enjoyed movies about American college life. And it was
these films that gave him the idea of studying in the United
States in the first place.

During the 1930s, Hollywood movie studios produced a
string of popular romantic comedies set on imaginary college campuses. In films like Ieoh Ming's favorite, *College
Humor*, starring Bing Crosby, American college life was por-
trayed as an endless round of football games, formal dances,
and light-hearted pranks. Pei realized that this carefree
version of U.S. college life probably had little basis in fact.
After all, the United States was then in the midst of the
major economic downturn known as the Great Depression,
meaning that most Americans fortunate enough to afford
college tuition were likely to be serious about their studies.
Even so, Ieoh Ming was drawn to the energetic and freewheel-
ing youth culture that the American movies depicted. "The
youth and freshness was one thing that came across, even
then in the thirties, whereas in China young people normally
were very reluctant to express themselves," Pei said about the
films as an adult. "In China people were more inclined to be
restrained. The States seemed to have a more easy-going lifestyle that was very appealing to me. . . . I decided that was the
country for me."

Yet, despite his enthusiasm for American culture and social
life, Ieoh Ming had no thought of staying in the United States
permanently. Deeply patriotic, he intended to use the knowl-
edge and skills he gained from his modern American education
to help turn his backward and exploited country into a strong
and respected world power.

By 1934, when I.M. turned 17, the political reunification
of China under Chiang Kai-shek and his Nationalist Party
had begun to fall apart. In some parts of the republic, fighting
had broken out between local Nationalist groups and former

warlords. Adding to Chiang Kai-shek's troubles, Communist commandos led by Mao Zedong established military bases in the Chinese countryside and won over thousands of local peasants to their cause. Because of these distractions, the Nationalist government proved unable to stand up either to continued Western interference in Shanghai and other Chinese ports or to a dangerous new threat from the East—the land-hungry and militaristic leaders of the Japanese Empire. From 1931 on, Japanese troops overran more and more of China's mineral-rich northern territories, until by mid-decade they had occupied a large portion of North China. (Communism is an economic and social system in which private property no longer exists and all of a country's resources and means of production are communally owned by the people.)

CHOOSING A COURSE OF STUDY

After deciding that he wanted to attend college in the United States, Ieoh Ming focused on choosing a major. Tsuyee urged him to study business or medicine. I.M. was determined to select his own career path, however. Ultimately, he settled on architecture, the art and science of designing and constructing buildings.

Pei's choice of a major was closely tied to his fascination with Shanghai's first skyscraper, the luxurious Park Hotel. Located across the street from I.M.'s favorite movie theater, the hotel was erected over a period of several months during his senior year in high school. Ieoh Ming watched in awe as the steel-frame building rose higher and higher, until finally it stood 24 floors tall. Shanghai's new skyscraper paled in comparison with New York City's towering skyscrapers, which by the early 1930s included the 102-story Empire State Building and the 77-story Chrysler Building. Yet the hotel was extremely impressive by Shanghai standards. On its completion in 1935, the Park Hotel was three times taller than the city's

In Shanghai, China, traffic zips by the Park Hotel, now dwarfed by other skyscrapers in the city. When it was completed in 1935, the 24-story Park Hotel was the tallest building in Shanghai by far, and it remained the highest building in China for more than three decades. The hotel fascinated young I.M. Pei, who decided to study architecture in the United States.

next-highest building. The hotel was also the tallest building in all of China, a distinction it would hold for more than 30 years. Excited by the thought of designing a building so grand, Ieoh Ming pored through St. John's big collection of American college catalogs, looking for schools with architecture programs. In the end, he decided to apply to the architecture department at the University of Pennsylvania in Philadelphia, or Penn, as the school is popularly known.

Tsuyee Pei was deeply disappointed by his son's choice of a major. He was even more displeased with Ieoh Ming's determination to attend an American college instead of Oxford. I.M.'s willingness to challenge his father's authority was daring. In keeping with the traditional Confucian emphasis on respect toward parents, most Chinese fathers expected strict obedience from their children. At Tsuyee's strong urging, I.M. did agree to take Oxford's demanding entrance exams. But even after he easily passed the difficult tests, Ieoh Ming stubbornly insisted that he was going to school in Philadelphia, with or without his father's blessing.

A NEW WORLD

In August 1935, I.M. Pei departed Shanghai for San Francisco, California, on the SS *President Coolidge* ocean liner. Even though he was setting out on a journey that would take him half a world away from his home, the 18-year-old did not feel sad as he waved goodbye to his family from the ship's deck. "I just thought about how lucky I was to have the opportunity to see a new world," he later reminisced. After nearly three weeks at sea, the *President Coolidge* finally entered San Francisco Bay. Pei's first glimpse of American soil from shipboard was an exhilarating experience. "When [San Francisco] appeared, it was a moment of great expectation and excitement. The sense of joy was unbelievable and difficult to describe," he could still vividly recall decades later.

After spending a few days in San Francisco taking in the sights, Pei boarded a train for Philadelphia and his new school. Pei's time at Penn would turn out to be short, however. The architecture department's emphasis on drawing made Pei deeply uncomfortable. He had never had any formal training in drawing and was sure that he lacked any natural talent for it. After spending just two weeks at Penn, Pei decided to cut his losses and find another architecture program.

Pei had recently met several Chinese students who attended the Massachusetts Institute of Technology (MIT) in Cambridge. They liked MIT and encouraged Pei to apply there. After discovering that MIT offered a specialized degree in architectural engineering, Pei decided to follow his new friends' advice and transfer to the school in the early autumn of 1935. As an architectural engineering student, Pei would learn to apply scientific and mathematic principles to the efficient construction of buildings. Convinced that he would never be able to draw well enough to be a successful designer, Pei figured he would be better off focusing on architecture's engineering side as opposed to its artistic aspects.

MIT AND MODERNISM

Pei entered MIT with every intention of specializing in architectural engineering. To his surprise, however, the school's dean of architecture, William Emerson, immediately decided that his new transfer student had a gift for design. When Pei tried to tell Emerson that he had no talent for art, the dean replied that such thinking was nonsense: It was a well-known fact that *all* Chinese could draw. In a recent interview, Pei recalled Emerson's wild generalization about the Chinese people's natural artistic abilities with amusement. "Of course it is not true, but it was his way of saying, 'Don't be discouraged, ... study architecture,'" Pei said. Buoyed by Emerson's faith in him, Pei decided to recommit himself to architectural design. From that point on, he never turned back.

Pei would later recall his years at MIT, from his arrival there in the fall of 1935 until his graduation in 1940, with great fondness. Nevertheless, as a student he was often frustrated by his teachers' conservative approach to architecture. In common with most other architecture programs of the time in the United States, MIT's program focused on the architectural styles of the past, especially the classical architecture of ancient Greece and Rome. Modernist architecture, a revolutionary new design movement that developed in Europe at the turn of the twentieth century, had no part in MIT's tradition-bound curriculum. Determined to learn everything he could about Modernism,

While attending the Massachusetts Institute of Technology, I.M. Pei became interested in Modernist architects like Walter Gropius and Le Corbusier. Above is the Villa Savoye in Poissy, France, designed by Le Corbusier in 1929. Buildings designed by the Modernists had little surface decoration and were often cubic in shape.

Pei spent countless hours holed up in the library, researching the works of the leading Modernist architects, including Walter Gropius of Germany and Pei's particular favorite, Le Corbusier (born Charles Édouard Jeanneret) of France.

During the 1930s, Le Corbusier, Gropius, and most other cutting-edge Modernist designers followed the so-called International Style of architecture, which first appeared in Germany around 1920. Like the larger Modernist movement of which it was a part, the International Style sought to break with past styles and techniques to create an entirely new type of architecture. Above all, this new kind of architecture was meant to reflect the spirit of the modern, industrialized age. Buildings in the International Style featured little or no surface decoration, cubic and other geometric shapes, open floor plans that emphasized function over form, and such modern materials as reinforced concrete, steel, and glass. The creative use of natural light was also stressed, especially in the works of Le Corbusier. Although Pei's conservative professors at MIT paid little attention to them, the ideas of Le Corbusier and other early leaders of the International Style were destined to have an enormous influence on Pei throughout his long architectural career.

MARRIAGE AND WORLD WAR II

In 1940, Pei received his bachelor of architecture degree from MIT. In recognition of his outstanding academic record, he was awarded several of the school's top architectural prizes, including a traveling fellowship. Pei would have liked to use the money provided by the fellowship to see the great architectural masterpieces of Europe. But World War II had erupted in Europe in late 1939, forcing him to put off his European travel plans indefinitely. Even more than he wanted to tour Europe in 1940, Pei wanted to go home to China, as he had always intended to do after earning his college degree. Because of the country's ever-widening war with Japan, however, his father

"PROPAGANDA UNITS
FOR THE CHINESE GOVERNMENT"

For his senior thesis project at MIT, I.M. Pei wanted to design something that could make some sort of meaningful contribution to his struggling homeland. "I was very nationalistic," he recently told an interviewer. "I wanted China to get stronger. China seemed so hopeless at that time." By late 1939, when Pei started his thesis project, a full-scale war between China and its imperialistic neighbor, Japan, had been raging for more than two years. Like many Chinese, Pei worried about how long China's forces would be able to hold out against the highly modernized Japanese army. According to Pei, however, it was not the war with Japan, but rather "the helplessness and ignorance" of his homeland's peasant masses that was at the heart of his "despair for China" in 1939.

During the 1930s, "85 percent of the [Chinese] population could not read or write. There were no newspapers outside of the big cities," Pei recently told an interviewer when asked about his choice of a senior thesis project. To try to deal with these problems, Pei decided to design a series of "prefabricated units built of bamboo where news and entertainment could be obtained, to be placed in remote villages and communities." Pei planned the lightweight bamboo "information" units so that they could be easily taken apart and transported from one rural town to another.

Pei's thesis adviser liked everything about his creative thesis project with one exception: its title, "Propaganda Units for the Chinese Government." Pei had labeled the movable units "propaganda units," not realizing that the word *propaganda* made many Americans uncomfortable because of its association with the Soviet Union's oppressive Communist government. Pei's adviser urged him to come up with another name for his thesis. Pei, who prided himself on his independence of mind, held his ground, however. For him, he insisted, the term *propaganda* simply meant "a kind of public education" and had no political undertones.

strongly urged him to stay away from China. The last several years had been stressful for Tsuyee Pei. In late 1937, he had been forced to flee Shanghai when the city fell to the Japanese army after a drawn-out, bloody battle. He settled in central China, in Nationalist leader Chiang Kai-shek's wartime capital of Chongqing, which was subjected to repeated Japanese air attacks. In light of his father's experiences, Pei decided that he had little choice but to remain in the United States for the time being. Shortly after graduating, he accepted a position with the Boston-based Bemis Foundation, which conducted research on housing, including the use of economical construction methods and building materials.

While with the Bemis Foundation, Pei became engaged to Eileen Loo, a young Chinese woman. (Eileen's original name was Ai-Ling Loo, but she decided to take an English first name before coming to the United States.) Loo had sailed to the United States from Hong Kong in 1938 to attend Wellesley College, a women's college near Boston. Pei and his fiancée had much in common, from their privileged upper-class upbringings to their deep love of architecture. Within a week of Loo's graduation from Wellesley in June 1942, Eileen and I.M. were wed in a ceremony performed by the Chinese consul to the United States, General James Yu. Shortly afterward, Eileen enrolled in a graduate program in landscape architecture at Harvard University in Cambridge, near MIT. (Landscape architecture is the science and art of arranging land, together with the buildings and other objects on it, for human use and enjoyment.)

In late 1942, Pei decided to join Eileen at Harvard. His goal was to earn a master's degree in architecture at the university's highly regarded Graduate School of Design. Pei was particularly drawn to the school's forward-looking faculty, including the world-renowned Modernist architects Walter Gropius and Marcel Breuer. Both men had come to the United States several years earlier as refugees from Nazi Germany. Despite his enthusiasm for his professors at Harvard, however, Pei put his studies on hold after two months to work for the U.S. government. His new employer was the National Defense Research

PEI AND THE NATIONAL DEFENSE RESEARCH COMMITTEE

When I.M. Pei volunteered his services to the U.S. National Defense Research Committee in January 1943, he was assigned to the division of the NDRC that focused on bomb-damage assessment and structural offense. One of Pei's first tasks was to study the structure of bridges and other buildings in Germany and Italy and then advise the military on the most efficient way to bomb them. "If you know how to build," Pei recalled his superiors in the NDRC telling him, "you should also know how to destroy."

In 1945, the final year of the war, Pei turned his attention from Europe to Japan. Leveling Japanese urban areas was very different from bombing German and Italian cities, where most buildings were constructed of brick and stone. Since "Japanese buildings at the time were mostly constructed of wood and paper," Pei later recalled, "the high explosives being used in Europe would not be very efficient." Consequently, Pei was asked to help develop an incendiary bomb for use in Japan instead. (Filled with a flammable substance, incendiary bombs are designed to start fires on impact.) Although eager to help bring the war to an end as quickly as possible, Pei nonetheless felt deeply uncomfortable about his role in helping to find more effective ways to incinerate enemy homes and workplaces. Even many decades after World War II, he was still clearly ambivalent about his work for the NDRC. "I would be brought photographs of Japanese towns," Pei told an interviewer recently, "and I was supposed to figure out the best way to burn them down. It was awful: I don't even like to think about it."

Committee (NDRC), formed by President Franklin D. Roosevelt in 1940 to organize scientific and technological research of interest to the U.S. armed forces.

On December 7, 1941, a devastating Japanese air attack on Pearl Harbor, Hawaii, had catapulted the United States into the Second World War. Ever since, Pei had been eager to contribute in some way to the U.S. military campaign against China's longtime enemy, Japan, and its chief allies, Germany and Italy. So, in January 1943, when Pei was invited to assist the NDRC in developing better strategies for destroying bridges and other structures in enemy territories, he jumped at the chance to be part of the American war effort. Pei's dream was that, once Japan was defeated and China was at peace again, he and Eileen would finally be able to return home to reunite with their families and help rebuild their shattered country.

4

Starting Out

The formal surrender of Japan to the Allied Powers, including the United States and China, on September 2, 1945, finally brought World War II to a close. I.M. and Eileen Pei could hardly wait to go home at long last. Once again, however, Tsuyee Pei urged his son to postpone his return because of unsettled conditions in China. Throughout most of the 1930s, the Nationalist government of Chiang Kai-shek had been locked in a bloody power struggle with the Communists under Mao Zedong. After full-scale war broke out between China and Japan in 1937, Mao and Chiang agreed to a cease-fire. With Japan's surrender, however, the fighting between the Nationalists and the Communists started up again with a vengeance. Until the violence ended, Ieoh Ming and Eileen should stay away from China, Tsuyee warned, especially now that they had a child to consider: their son T'ing Chung, born in 1944.

BACK TO HARVARD

In the autumn of 1945, his work for the U.S. National Defense Research Committee done, Pei went back to his studies at Harvard's Graduate School of Design. In recognition of his outstanding abilities as a designer, Pei was also hired to teach a design studio class at the Graduate School. This was an unusual honor, since Pei had not yet earned his master's degree. According to one former student, Pei "was an inspiring teacher: He immediately understood what you were trying to do and helped you articulate it."

Pei was excited to be back at Harvard, studying under two of the best-known and respected Modernist architects of the day, Marcel Breuer of Hungary and the School of Design's director, Walter Gropius. "Gropius represented to me an opportunity to see the new," Pei would later say of his famous professor. Yet, despite his appreciation for Gropius's forward-looking approach, that "didn't mean that I agreed with him always and on every point," Pei added. In particular, Pei doubted Gropius's claim that the spread of industrialization through the world would soon create a single, "international" style of architecture. "What about the relationship between history and architecture; between culture and architecture; climate and architecture?" Pei recalled asking Gropius. "It was at that moment that I said I would like to prove something to myself, that there is a limit to the internationalization of architecture," he reminisced. "It was very important for Harvard to know . . . that there are cultural differences that should be expressed in architecture."

Pei hoped to use his master's thesis project to try to prove his point about the importance of a country's unique culture and history for architectural design. For his thesis topic, he chose to create a plan for an art museum in his old hometown, Shanghai. Pei designed the building in the Modernist, or International Style, favored by Gropius and Breuer, with a cubic shape and very little surface decoration. He wanted his project to reflect

After World War II, I.M. Pei returned to the Graduate School of Design at Harvard University. The director of the school was the famed Modernist architect Walter Gropius. Here, Gropius posed with a draft of one of his projects, an entry in the design competition for the Chicago Tribune building.

Chinese culture in some way, but without relying on widely recognized Chinese architectural details, like the tiled roofs with upturned edges found on many buildings in his homeland. To give a Chinese character to his museum, he decided to surround the building with many small gardens, in keeping with the Chinese tradition that "art and gardens are inseparable." Pei placed the gardens, including a larger central one with a stream, so that their ornamental trees and shrubs could be seen from almost anywhere within the museum. "All forms of Chinese art are directly or indirectly results of a sensitive observation of nature. Such objects, consequently, are best displayed in surroundings which are in tune with them, surroundings which incorporate as much as possible the controlling elements of natural beauty," he explained.

Pei's design was well received by his professors. Breuer even went as far as to call it the most important thesis project produced by a School of Design student. Gropius praised Pei for skillfully bringing together the new and the old as well as Western and Eastern in his museum plan. Pei's blueprint "clearly illustrates that an able designer can very well hold on to basic traditional features—which he has found are still alive—without sacrificing a progressive conception of design," he wrote. Upon Pei's graduation in 1946, Gropius immediately offered his star student a full-time teaching position in the School of Design. Ieoh Ming and Eileen still dreamed of returning to China with their family, which now included a second son, Chien Chung. But with the civil war between the Nationalists and the Communists showing no signs of ending, Pei decided to accept Gropius's offer and stay in Cambridge for the time being.

AN UNUSUAL CAREER PATH

Pei remained at the Graduate School of Design as an assistant professor for two years after earning his master's degree in architecture. Then, in 1948, he decided to take an unusual career path for a young architect just starting out. While most of his classmates were trying to build up their résumés by designing vacation homes or house additions for relatives or friends, Pei went to work for one of the most successful real estate tycoons in America, William Zeckendorf.

Zeckendorf was the larger-than-life owner and president of Webb & Knapp, New York City's top real estate company. Standing six feet tall (183 centimeters) and weighing 250 pounds (113 kilograms), Zeckendorf "was a big man in just about every way," Carter Wiseman observed in *I.M. Pei: A Profile in American Architecture*. Zeckendorf loved big limousines, big cigars, big parties, and, most of all, big real estate deals. At its high point, his real estate empire reportedly included "20,000 apartments, 10 million square feet of office space, 6,500 hotel rooms, and assorted other holdings worth some $300 million," Wiseman wrote. By the late 1940s, however, Zeckendorf had become increasingly restless. He wanted to do more than just buy and sell urban real estate: He wanted to oversee the construction of great urban buildings as well. So Zeckendorf decided to give his company something that very few other real estate development firms had at the time: its own architectural design division. To head the division, Zeckendorf sought a fresh young design talent with a strong background in Modernist architecture. In early 1948, an acquaintance on the staff of the Museum of Modern Art in New York suggested that Zeckendorf interview a brilliant 30-year-old professor at the Harvard School of Design for the job. His name was I.M. Pei.

When Zeckendorf interviewed Pei, he was bowled over by the young professor's remarkable drive, intelligence, and self-confidence. Even though Pei had little real-world experience as an architect, Zeckendorf was absolutely convinced that he was the best person for the job. When he asked Pei to serve as his new director of architectural research, however, Pei was torn by the offer. On the one hand, he admired Zeckendorf's enormous

I.M. Pei taught for two years at Harvard and then took the unusual step of joining the real estate firm of Webb & Knapp, headed by the flamboyant William Zeckendorf *(above, left)*. Zeckendorf wanted to undertake large-scale urban projects, and Pei joined the firm as its director of architectural research.

energy and willingness to think "on the grand scale." He also liked the idea of learning more about real estate, since "to be an architect in China, unlike here, you've got to know real estate," Pei later explained to an interviewer. On the other hand, he was not sure that he wanted to give up teaching, which he genuinely enjoyed. Moreover, he worried whether moving to New York City would be fair to Eileen, who had put her career on hold several years earlier to be at home full time with their young children. If Eileen wanted to return to work, she would have a better chance of finding employment as a landscape architect in the Cambridge area than in New York, he thought. But Eileen supported the move, and in the end, Zeckendorf's pledge to Pei "that the kind of things we were going to do would be so different and so much better than anyone else in the country was doing" proved impossible to resist. In the fall of 1948, the Peis moved to a small apartment in Manhattan, and I.M. began what would turn out to be a 12-year partnership with Webb & Knapp and its colorful owner.

REBUILDING AMERICA'S CITIES

During his first years with Webb & Knapp, Pei spent much of his time traveling with his boss to cities across the United States, scouting out new building projects. Zeckendorf was extremely eager to take part in the urban-renewal movement then sweeping the United States. Many of the country's largest cities had deteriorated badly during the Great Depression (1929–1939) and World War II. After the war, the federal government decided that something must be done to make America's decaying urban areas better places in which to live and work. Congress voted to provide federal money for local authorities to identify particularly run-down areas in their cities, buy the land, and clear it. Private real estate developers like Zeckendorf would then present their plans for rebuilding the bulldozed areas to the mayor and other city officials. Should the officials decide to approve a developer's proposal for rebuilding a cleared area, he or she would be given the opportunity to purchase the land at a bargain price.

After identifying a city that seemed like a good candidate for redevelopment, Zeckendorf and Pei would head there on Webb & Knapp's small private airplane. When they arrived, Zeckendorf would typically order the pilot to circle low over the city, so that he and his head architect could study it firsthand before meeting with local officials and business and community leaders. At the meetings, Pei presented his and Zeckendorf's ambitious plans for rebuilding run-down sections of the city with modern office complexes, low-cost public-housing units, recreational facilities, and other types of structures. Pei's intelligence, creativity, and enthusiasm made a positive impression on his audiences, helping Webb & Knapp secure a number of important urban-renewal projects in cities across the United States. Pei's use of elegantly made wood models in his presentations instead of the usual architectural drawings was also a great help to Webb & Knapp in beating out rivals for redevelopment jobs. "What makes I.M. and his crew different from other architects," one Boston city planner observed, "is that they are so articulate and clear-sighted in matters that govern urban redevelopment. . . . They build these detailed scale models of whole sectors of the city, and these models demonstrate to any laymen the implications of a given project—much more clearly than the drawings ever could."

Zeckendorf had good reason to be pleased with his decision to make Pei his chief architect in 1948, despite the young professor's almost complete lack of experience outside the academic world. Pei, too, found much to be grateful for in his professional partnership with Zeckendorf. He had gone to work for Webb & Knapp in order to learn about real estate. In the end, what he learned about architecture's political side would prove even more important to his future. Pei's years with Zeckendorf gave him an extraordinary opportunity to design large-scale projects with large-scale budgets to match—"to think big," as he put it. But the single most useful thing he learned from his Webb & Knapp days, Pei later recalled, was that "good ideas are worth nothing without good allies who support them." Again and again during his career, and especially in his challenging campaign to win support for his famous addition to the Louvre, Pei would find himself relying on the political skills he developed while pitching his and Zeckendorf's urban-renewal proposals to government and business leaders across the United States.

DENVER'S MILE HIGH CENTER

Pei's first big design project as architecture director for Webb & Knapp was a Modernist, high-rise office tower in downtown Denver. Begun in 1952, the 23-story building was named the Mile High Center, in honor of the fact that Denver is exactly one mile (1.61 kilometers) above sea level. After World War II, as was true in many American cities, Denver's booming population pushed out into its suburbs, while the city's downtown became more and more dilapidated. Indeed, there had been no new construction of any significance in downtown Denver since before the start of the Great Depression. Seeing an opportunity, in 1945 Zeckendorf purchased several acres of land in the heart of Denver, near the busiest retail strip. After he hired Pei, the two began to plan a major office, shopping, and entertainment complex on the land, of which the Mile High office tower was to be the first phase.

Pei's design for the Mile High Center was quite unusual for its time. For one thing, Pei raised the office tower on stilts and set it back from the street to create a spacious plaza—an open, public area, where workers and pedestrians could stroll or relax. The plaza, which took up much of the 2.5-acre (1-hectare) building site, featured patterned pavement, piped-in music, trees, flowerbeds, illuminated fountains, and a 200-foot-long (61-meter) refrigerated pool stocked with mountain trout. Almost no commercial buildings in the United States had plazas when Pei began to design the Mile High Center. That quickly changed after the center and its beautifully landscaped courtyard opened to enormous public and critical acclaim in 1956.

Another groundbreaking feature of the Mile High Center was its richly textured façade. (A façade is the face of a building.) By the 1950s, rectangular skyscrapers composed of steel frames filled in with great sheets of glass had become the most common type of Modernist architecture in the United States. What set the Mile High Center apart from these plain glass boxes was that, instead of the usual unadorned Modernist glass wall, its façade was arranged into a complex basket-weave pattern that emphasized the building's different functional elements. Philip Jodidio and Janet Adams Strong described Pei's unique design for the center's exterior in their book, *I.M. Pei, Complete Works*:

> Its tapestry-like curtain wall traces the structural skeleton with dark gray aluminum panels, while beige enamel "threads" interweave the horizontal heating/cooling units under each window and the narrower vertical air ducts. Between the window units and floors, 12-inch-wide (30-centimeter) fixed glass ribbons dramatize, especially at night, the depth of its deceptively flat walls.

The Mile High Center, promoted by Zeckendorf as "the most progressive building between San Francisco and Chicago," was a huge hit with Denver's citizens and popular press alike. Architectural journals also heaped praise on the center, especially for its creative and eye-catching façade and plaza. Traditionally, architectural critics looked down on designers who worked for big real estate developers like Zeckendorf. But the Denver project allowed Pei and his growing design team, which now included two other young Harvard graduates, Henry Cobb and Araldo Cossutta, to establish themselves as something more than just "run-of-the mill commercial architects," Carter Wiseman wrote. After the Mile High Center opened in 1956, "we were no longer just a bunch of university guys, a group of youngsters," Pei later said about the Webb & Knapp design team.

BECOMING A U.S. CITIZEN

In 1955, as the Mile High Center was nearing completion, I.M. and Eileen Pei made a difficult decision. They decided to give up all hopes of returning home to China and became citizens of the United States.

In late 1949, Communist forces under Mao Zedong finally defeated their Nationalist enemies led by Chiang Kai-shek, who soon fled to the island of Taiwan. Like many other prosperous Chinese businesspeople and professionals, Tsuyee Pei did not want to live under a Communist economic system. Because Mao and his followers had always stressed that anyone who was not with them was against them, Tsuyee also feared that his support for the Nationalists during the civil war would lead to his imprisonment or even execution by the Maoists. After Mao officially proclaimed the founding of the Communist People's Republic of China in October 1949,

USING NATURE TO COPE WITH HOMESICKNESS

During the early 1950s, I.M. Pei designed and built a small house in the hills of Katonah, outside of New York City, where his growing family could escape from the city on weekends. To remind them of their homeland, I.M. and Eileen planted Chinese pine trees and a Chinese-style garden near the house. Over the years, Pei later reflected, the garden and trees played an important role in helping him cope with his homesickness for his birth country:

> We created a little garden—very small but very Chinese—with some grasses and flowers which reminded us of China. My love for gardening probably has its roots in that time. . . .
>
> Nature and man working together, that is in my blood and I brought it from China. That is why working with nature helped me to overcome the loss of my country to a certain extent.

Communist troops marched past the Park Hotel in Shanghai, China, after occupying the city in June 1949. The Communists defeated the Nationalists that year to take control of the country. By 1955, I.M. Pei and his wife realized that they would not be able to return to their homeland, and they became U.S. citizens.

therefore, Tsuyee, along with a number of other family members, left the mainland for Hong Kong. At that time, Hong Kong was still under British rule (and would remain so until 1997). In Hong Kong, Tsuyee used his strong background in English and foreign exchange to build a successful career as an international banker. Because his work frequently brought him to New York, Tsuyee was able to renew his relationship with his eldest son and finally become acquainted with his grandsons, T'ing Chung, Chien Chung (Didi), and Li Chung (Sandi), born in 1950. (Eileen and Ieoh Ming's fourth and last child, daughter Liane, was born in 1960.) Eventually, Tsuyee decided to move to New York City permanently.

By the mid-1950s, when Eileen and I.M. decided to renounce their Chinese citizenship, Mao was firmly entrenched in power, and it was clear that his regime was every bit as brutal and oppressive as Tsuyee had feared. From 1949 to 1955, the Maoists executed an estimated 1 million Chinese whom they suspected of opposing their policies and sent another 2 million to labor camps for "re-education." Tens of thousands of the detainees never made it out of the bleak labor camps, the victims of disease, overwork, malnutrition, or suicide. Giving up their Chinese citizenship was emotionally painful for the Peis, but living under Mao's tyrannical rule was clearly out of the question. Moreover, as I.M. told an interviewer years later, the Pei children were "totally Americans." They had spent their entire lives in the United States, attending American schools, making American friends, and speaking nothing but English, even with their parents. Consequently, they looked on the United States, not China, as their true homeland, and they very much wanted to stay there.

On Veterans Day, November 11, 1955, Eileen and Ieoh Ming Pei took the U.S. citizenship oath at New York City's Polo Grounds along with 10,000 other immigrants from around the globe. (Since they were born on American soil, the Pei children were already U.S. citizens.) Years later, Pei reflected on his emotional state that November day and on the consequences of his decision to become an American citizen:

> On the one hand, feelings of sorrow at having to abandon our culture, our roots, our ancestral home. On the other hand, feelings of gratitude—more than happiness—that we have this wonderful country in which to live. . . .
>
> America has been a blessing to me. It has given me a dimension of challenge which I don't think I would have been able to experience anywhere else. For me, this is a country to which I owe nearly everything I have.

5

Pei Makes a Name for Himself

In 1955, the year that I.M. Pei became a U.S. citizen, he also founded his own architectural partnership, I.M. Pei & Associates (renamed I.M. Pei & Partners in 1966 and Pei, Cobb, Freed & Partners in 1989). By the mid-1950s, Webb & Knapp's architecture division had grown to include 70 people. Pei thought it was time to give his senior designers—and himself—a professional identity apart from Webb & Knapp. For the first nearly five years of the new firm's existence, however, I.M. Pei & Associates continued to work only on projects for William Zeckendorf.

SOCIETY HILL

I.M. Pei & Associates' most important projects for Zeckendorf and his development company were two large urban-housing developments. The first was in the Society Hill district of one of America's most historic and beloved cities, Philadelphia.

In the late 1950s, the city of Philadelphia held a national competition for developer-architect teams to come up with an urban-renewal plan for the city's historic Society Hill neigh-borhood. Located along the Delaware River in Center City Philadelphia, Society Hill had been one of the city's most fashionable residential areas during the eighteenth and early nineteenth centuries. By the early 1900s, though, it had become home to a sprawling wholesale produce market and smoke-belching factories, and its once elegant homes had fallen into disrepair. Most urban-renewal projects of the 1950s and '60s involved bulldozing entire areas and starting from scratch. Philadelphia officials did not want to do that in Society Hill. Instead, they planned to tear down the area's unsightly factories and warehouses while preserving as many of its historic buildings as possible. In place of the demolished factories and warehouses, they wanted to construct an attractive and modern housing complex to lure Philadelphians back to the decaying neighborhood. The challenge they presented to the developer-architect teams who entered the Society Hill competition was to design a housing complex that retained the neighborhood's historic flavor by successfully melding the modern with the old.

Pei was thrilled when I.M. Pei & Associates and Zeckendorf beat out several better-known designer-developer teams in 1957 to win the national contest for Society Hill's new housing complex. Pei's winning proposal called for three concrete, high-rise apartment towers to be built on the crest of the hill, set back from the area's older homes, churches, and other structures. Additional housing in the form of several dozen single-family row houses was to be constructed along the borders of Society Hill's historic sections. In his plan, Pei gracefully blended new and old, as city officials had called for, through a number of different strategies. For example, he carefully positioned the slender, 31-story apartment towers so that they would frame views of historic landmarks such as graceful Christ Church, built in 1695. He also made a point of designing the single-family row houses with their historic neighbors in mind. Although the townhouses were clearly modern, they complemented nearby eighteenth-century buildings in their scale, style of windows and doorways, and building materials (chiefly brick and limestone). Nearly a half-century after the project's completion in 1964, Pei still considers Society Hill one of his proudest accomplishments.

KIPS BAY

The same year that they won the Society Hill competition, Pei and Zeckendorf began to collaborate on another major urban-housing project, this one in New York City. Located on a three-block site in East Manhattan called Kips Bay, the new project would give Pei and his design team a reputation for superior technical know-how and innovation that set them apart from most other architectural firms of the period.

Since Kips Bay was a government-funded public-housing project, Pei had to work on a tight budget in designing and constructing the complex. Most of the dreary, cookie-cutter public-housing projects built in U.S. cities during the 1950s could hardly be described as good architecture. Pei, however, was determined to use Kips Bay to prove that even low-cost urban housing could be attractive and imaginative. Instead of taking up most of the 10-acre (4-hectare) site with six separate buildings, as originally suggested, he consolidated all 1,000 of the project's housing units into twin, 21-story towers. This left nearly half of the site empty. Pei then positioned the twin rectangular slabs so that they created a sheltered park out of the leftover acreage. In the park, which proved very popular with the housing project's tenants, Pei planted 50 young trees. He also asked Zeckendorf for permission to buy a large, modern sculpture by the famous Spanish artist Pablo Picasso for the park. Zeckendorf turned him down, saying that their budget for the project was too small for such a purchase.

I.M. Pei used the innovative technique of cast-in-place concrete for the apartment buildings at Kips Bay Plaza in Manhattan. With his design, which included a sheltered park, Pei demonstrated that low-cost urban housing could also be attractive.

Including a spacious, private park in an urban public-housing project was certainly innovative. But it was Pei's groundbreaking use of cast-in-place concrete to construct the two apartment buildings that really captured the attention of the architectural community. Cast-in-place concrete is cast—or molded—in a form at the building site before being placed into its final position on a structure. At Kips Bay, Pei revealed his technical expertise and originality by doing something that had never been done before in a concrete high-rise. He assembled his twin skyscrapers by stacking cast-in-place concrete window frames one on top of the other like giant blocks. The structure created by this new system was attractive in a rugged sort of way and also relatively cheap to make, since it could be constructed quickly and required neither an expensive steel frame nor an exterior brick "skin" or façade. For Pei's innovative construction technique, specially formulated lightweight, beige cement along with sand and crushed stone were poured into a fiberglass and wooden form that had been designed according to Pei's precise specifications. "And what came out of the form was the building itself: fireproof structure, façade, window frame, and finish, interior and exterior, all molded together in an honest whole, with nothing hidden or added," authors Philip Jodidio and Janet Adams Strong wrote. "Within the dull economic formula for urban renewal, Kips Bay was an attempt to transform large-scale city housing into architecture."

NEW DIRECTIONS AND NEW CHALLENGES

By 1960, Pei had worked for Zeckendorf for more than a decade. He felt fortunate to have had the opportunity to collaborate with the real estate tycoon on Society Hill, Kips Bay, and scores of other large-scale housing and commercial-development projects. But Pei was impatient to take on new kinds of design challenges, including art museums, concert halls, and other public buildings. After consulting with his staff at I.M. Pei & Associates, Pei broke the news to Zeckendorf that the firm had decided to seek new clients. In a gracious farewell letter to Pei dated August 1, 1960, Zeckendorf wrote: "It is more than twelve years since Ieoh Ming Pei became associated with Webb & Knapp. . . . Together we have . . . passed many milestones that will be looked upon by future writers of the contemporary scene as having perhaps had a profound effect upon American construction and the way of life that emanates from good design."

Just 10 months after breaking with Zeckendorf, Pei received one of the most exciting and challenging assignments of his entire architectural career. In 1961, he was chosen to design the National Center for Atmospheric Research (NCAR) at the base of the Rocky Mountains near Boulder, Colorado. NCAR's new director, Dr. Walter Orr Roberts, had personally chosen the secluded site atop a 600-foot (183-meter) mesa for the new scientific research center. (Commonly found in the Southwestern United States, a mesa is a flat, elevated area with one or more cliff-like sides.)

Pei, who had only designed buildings for urban settings until this point, was awed by the site's wild beauty. Yet, at the same time, he found the immense scale of the mountains that formed its backdrop intimidating. "It was infinite; there was no scale," he later said of the NCAR site. "It was so completely different from urban architecture where nothing stands alone and where every building relates to other buildings and streets and plazas and the spaces between." Accompanied by Roberts, Pei explored every inch of the windswept site, trying to get a sense of the sort of building that could successfully "co-exist with the powerful scale of nature" on the mesa. He also returned several times by himself to study the mesa, even spending one night camping out under the stars in a sleeping bag. Being alone in the foothills of the Rockies brought back memories of his childhood trips with his mother to mountaintop Buddhist retreats. "There in the Colorado mountains, I tried to listen to the silence again—just as my mother had taught me," Pei recalled. "The investigation of the place became a kind of religious experience for me."

CREATING NCAR

Over a period of several months, Pei developed and quickly rejected a dozen design schemes for the NCAR facility. Finally, during a car trip through Colorado with Eileen, he hit upon a solution to the problem of how to keep the mesa's vast open spaces and mountainous background from overwhelming the new research center. The NCAR complex, he decided, must somehow join with its spectacular surroundings, rather than try to compete with them. The inspiration for Pei's new approach came from ancient Native American cliff dwellings he and Eileen visited in Mesa Verde National Park in southern Colorado. Built more than 600 years earlier, the simple mud-and-stone dwellings were tucked into the sides of the steep cliffs. In keeping with the Indians' belief that humankind should live in harmony with nature, the homes blended in so well with their ruggedly dramatic setting that they almost looked as if they "were carved out of the mountain," Pei later recalled.

The National Center for Atmospheric Research, set on a mesa near Boulder, Colorado, was I.M. Pei's first project outside of an urban setting. He mixed crushed stone from nearby mountains into the concrete so that the color of the building would resemble that of the surrounding peaks.

One reason the Pueblo dwellings actually appeared to be one with the cliffs, Pei believed, was that they had been made from local stone taken from the mountains themselves. Pei had already decided to construct the NCAR complex from concrete, since only a very strong building material could hold up to the 150-mile–per-hour (241-kilometer-per-hour) winds that sometimes swept across the mesa. Now he decided to mix crushed stone excavated from nearby mountains into the concrete. His strategy for joining the new science center to its mountain environment through its building materials proved a great success. When the NCAR facility was finally completed in 1967, its pinkish-brown shade so closely resembled the color of the surrounding peaks that, from a distance, the complex seemed to disappear right into the mountains.

Finding a way to make the new building complex blend in with its mountain backdrop was not the only challenge that Pei faced in designing NCAR. Roberts, the center's director, wanted the facility to be a place where scientists could easily come together to exchange ideas and information yet could also work alone. To translate Roberts's vision into architecture, Pei put the scientists' laboratories in a series of tall, narrow towers topped by "crow's nests," small private offices where researchers could engage in quiet contemplation amid magnificent views of nature. Since Roberts believed that chance meetings amongst scientists encouraged creativity and led to new discoveries, Pei also placed outdoor patios with benches; broad, winding staircases and hallways; and welcoming conversation alcoves throughout the complex.

Roberts and his staff of scientists at NCAR along with most of the country's leading architectural critics praised Pei's innovative and boldly modern design for the complex when it officially opened in 1967. Pei himself was not entirely satisfied with the completed research center, however. He would have liked to add another cluster of towers to the complex, but the project's budget would not permit it. Still, he was deeply grateful for the opportunity that NCAR gave him to explore the artistic side of architecture, something he had been able to do very little of during his years with William Zeckendorf.

THE JOHN F. KENNEDY LIBRARY

In 1964, three years after he was chosen to design NCAR, Pei received one of the most sought-after architectural commissions of the twentieth century. He was selected to design the John F. Kennedy Presidential Library in Cambridge, Massachusetts. In October 1963, President Kennedy, or JFK, as he was affectionately nicknamed by the American public, had obtained a two-acre (0.8-hectare) site at Harvard University for his future presidential library. Just one month later, Kennedy was cut down by an assassin's bullet as he and his wife, Jacqueline, rode in an open motorcar through the streets of Dallas, Texas. The national outpouring of grief for the charismatic 46-year-old president and of sympathy for his young widow was enormous. So, when Jacqueline Kennedy announced just two months after the assassination that planning had begun for a combined John F. Kennedy Library and memorial in Cambridge, the American people and press took a deep interest in the project.

Mrs. Kennedy asked a committee of leading designers from around the world to recommend an architect for the library and memorial. Among their top six choices was Pei. Over the next several months, Mrs. Kennedy met personally with all six architects to discuss her ideas and goals for the project. Although Pei was the least known and experienced of the group, she was drawn to his refreshing modesty and artistic and intellectual open-mindedness. She also liked his strong commitment to achieving harmony between his designs and their surrounding landscapes. "He didn't seem to have just one way to solve a problem," she said of Pei. "He seemed to approach each commission thinking only of it and then develop a way to make something beautiful." By the end of their second meeting, Jacqueline Kennedy had decided to award Pei the commission.

When Mrs. Kennedy's brother-in-law, Robert Kennedy, announced Pei's selection as the designer of the John F. Kennedy Library at a news conference on December 13, 1964, the 47-year-old Chinese-American architect became an instant celebrity. New commissions began to pour into I.M. Pei & Associates, and the young firm grew and prospered. In the meantime, Pei focused on developing a blueprint for the Kennedy Library, to which the Kennedy family now wanted to add a museum, a School of Government, and an Institute of Politics. Knowing how eager the American people were to have a fitting memorial to their fallen president, he hoped to have the ambitious project done within five years. Little could he have imagined that it would take three times that long for the library to be completed.

During the decade after JFK's death, Pei encountered one roadblock after another in designing and building his presidential library, starting with its location on Harvard's campus. Pei believed that the two-acre site that John Kennedy had secured from the university shortly before his death in 1963 was too small for a building that now had to serve as a memorial, museum, educational institution, public policy institute, and library, all wrapped into one. After many unexpected delays and complications, a larger plot of land in Cambridge was finally obtained for the building from the Commonwealth of Massachusetts. By the time the plot had been cleared and prepared for construction, many Cambridge residents had begun to turn against the project, complaining that it would attract hordes of tourists to their peaceful community. Moreover, they disliked Pei's proposed design for the library, especially the unusual, 85-foot-high (26-meter-high), truncated glass pyramid that was to serve as the building's centerpiece.

In response to the growing public criticism, Pei unveiled a new, scaled-down design for the library in 1974, minus the truncated glass pyramid. He was unhappy about having to change his design, but his first priority was to get the library built. Yet, despite the new design, many Cambridge residents

BOSTON'S JOHN HANCOCK TOWER

While I.M. Pei was struggling with his critics in Cambridge regarding the design and location of the John F. Kennedy Library, his architectural firm was facing another major public-relations challenge in nearby Boston. In 1967, Pei's partner, Henry Cobb, had begun to design a 60-story office tower for the John Hancock Mutual Life Insurance Company in downtown Boston. At 790 feet high (241 meters high), the John Hancock Tower was to be the tallest building in all of New England. This did not sit well with some Bostonians, who worried that the skyscraper would overwhelm its historic neighbors, including elegant Trinity Church, which stood adjacent to it. To address this issue, Cobb clad the entire tower in reflective glass and carefully positioned the building so that its prism-like walls mirrored the church's ornate façade.

In 1973, while the Hancock Tower was still under construction, disaster struck. High winds caused dozens of the building's large glass windows to shatter and fall to the sidewalk below. Fortunately, nobody was hurt, but over the next several months, whenever the winds picked up, more and more of the tower's windowpanes would develop ominous cracks. Soon, ugly plywood panels covered nearly one-third of its window units, earning the tower the insulting nickname of "Plywood Palace." With his firm's good name in jeopardy, Pei announced that all of the building's 10,000 windows would be replaced at a cost of some $7 million. Once the problem of the faulty windows had been solved, Bostonians slowly warmed to their new Modernist skyscraper. Today, the sleek glass tower is one of the city's most famous and beloved architectural landmarks.

I.M. Pei's stature rose with his selection in 1964 to design the John F. Kennedy Library. Several obstacles delayed the project, including opposition from residents of Cambridge, Massachusetts—the original site of the library. Finally, in 1979, the library and museum opened on Columbia Point near Boston Harbor.

continued to oppose the project, complaining that the memorial would forever change their quiet and historic town. Volunteering his own time, Pei devoted countless hours to try to drum up support for the library at one community meeting after another, but with discouraging results. "As long as JFK's blood remained vivid in the American memory," author Michael Cannell wrote, "mountains could have been moved on his behalf." By this point, however, it had been more than 10 years since the president's assassination, and "the project had by now squandered much of its precious impetus," Cannell observed.

In 1975, the president's widow (who had remarried and become Jacqueline Kennedy Onassis) finally decided to give up on Cambridge altogether and find a new location for the memorial. Four years later, on October 20, 1979, the new John F. Kennedy Library officially opened on Columbia Point, a remote spit of land southeast of Cambridge on Boston Harbor. The Modernistic building, which features a below-ground museum and a soaring 110-foot-high (33.5-meter-high) memorial pavilion, was well received by the people of Boston and most of the architectural community. Pei, however, was disappointed with the results of what had turned out to be the longest—and, in many ways, most frustrating—assignment of his architectural career. Somewhere in the course of the 15-year battle to build the library, he later admitted, "I lost my spirit. I couldn't give anymore. . . . The whole project was for me tragic. It could have been so great."

6

Pei's Two Greatest Triumphs

Until the opening of his famous glass pyramid expansion to the Louvre in 1989, I.M. Pei's most widely known and admired design was the East Building of the National Gallery of Art in Washington, D.C. Completed in 1978, the Modernist East Building's extraordinary knife-edge triangles and soaring interior spaces firmly established Pei as America's leading architect.

BEGINNINGS

The National Gallery of Art first came into being in 1937, when Congress authorized its construction on the National Mall in Washington, D.C. The capital's newest museum was the brainchild of businessman and philanthropist Andrew W. Mellon, one of the richest men in America and an enthusiastic art collector. (Philanthropists try to increase the well-being of others, usually through donations or charitable aid.) Mellon donated the heart of the gallery's holdings—nearly 150 European masterpieces from his personal collection—along with the money to construct the building. Sadly, he never got the chance to see his dream of a great national art museum fulfilled. Several months after Congress approved the gallery, Mellon died, leaving his son Paul to guide the museum to completion. Finished in 1941, the National Gallery was designed by John Russell Pope in the neoclassical style, a style of architecture inspired by the classical monuments of ancient Greece and Rome. Like Pope's more famous Washington, D.C., building, the Jefferson Memorial, the National Gallery had tall columns holding up a wide portico and a massive domed roof. (A portico is a columned porch or walkway that generally leads to the entrance of a building.)

During the 1960s, Paul Mellon, a member of the National Gallery's Board of Trustees since his father's death and the museum's president, decided the time had come to enlarge the institution. The gallery's art holdings as well as its administrative and conservation staffs had grown significantly over the previous 20 years, and the museum was running out of space. (The conservation staff of an art museum is responsible for restoring and preserving its works of art.) The museum's administrators were particularly concerned about the lack of new exhibition space for the gallery's expanding collection of twentieth-century art. They also dreamed of making the museum into a national center of art research and scholarship by adding lecture halls and a much larger library and photography archives.

Mellon, who had agreed to pay for the expansion along with his sister, began to look for an architect in 1967. Mellon interviewed a half-dozen architects, but from the start, he favored Pei. Mellon particularly admired Pei's National Center for Atmospheric Research in Boulder, which had officially opened that same year. What finally persuaded Mellon to offer Pei the National Gallery commission was a Modernist art museum that Pei had recently designed in Syracuse, New York. Traditionally, architects designed art museums as monumental, almost temple-like containers for artworks. In Syracuse, though, Pei had taken a different approach. He designed the city's new Everson Museum as a finely crafted piece of modern sculpture. In effect, Pei made the museum building itself into a work of art, and that was exactly what Mellon had in mind for the National Gallery expansion.

TRAPEZOIDS AND TRIANGLES

When Pei was officially awarded the National Gallery commission in 1968, he quickly decided against attaching a wing to the existing structure. Instead, he resolved to construct a second building directly across from Pope's structure on an 8.8-acre (3.6-hectare) plot of land that Andrew Mellon had secured for the National Gallery back in the 1930s. Since it would be located to the east of the original museum building, Pei's new structure was dubbed the East Building. Even though Pope's building and most of the Mall's other monumental structures had been designed in the neoclassical style, Pei wanted the East Building to be Modernist. Yet achieving harmony between the National Gallery's newer and older parts was important to him. So that the two structures would be similar in color and texture, he sheathed the East Building in pinkish marble mined from the same Tennessee quarry that had provided the marble for the Pope building's façade 30 years earlier. Eventually, Pei decided to link the two buildings through a vast underground passageway containing, among other things, an auditorium, conservation workshops, storage areas, a gift shop, and a restaurant.

The single greatest challenge Pei faced in designing the East Building was the awkward, trapezoidal shape of its site at the intersection of Constitution and Pennsylvania avenues. "A conventional, rectangular structure was out of the question" on the oddly shaped plot, as author Carter Wiseman explained: "For one thing, it would have wasted a great deal of space at the unoccupied corners. For another, the axis through the center of such a building would have been off-center with the axis of

In designing the East Building of the National Gallery of Art in Washington, D.C., I.M. Pei had to solve the problem of placing a building on an oddly shaped tract of land. To do so, he created two triangular sections connected by a soaring, sky-lit central atrium.

the Pope building, and all agreed that there should be a symmetrical relationship between the two façades across the strip of Fourth Street that separated them." (An axis is a straight line with respect to which an object or figure is symmetrical.) After puzzling over the problem for weeks, Pei had a sudden inspiration. The trapezoidal site could be split into two triangular sections, he realized. One triangular section, he eventually decided, would house a series of small exhibition spaces stacked in towers. The other would house new administrative offices and a large research library and photographic archive.

To connect the East Building's triangular wings, Pei used another triangle, this one in the form of a soaring, sky-lit central court or atrium. Bridged by two catwalks, the four-story atrium evolved into one of the East Building's most dramatic and admired spaces. (A catwalk is a narrow, elevated walkway.) The lofty atrium serves both as a popular gathering place and as an exhibition gallery for large works of art, including a 76-foot-long (23-meter-long) mobile by Alexander Calder. Calder's brilliant red mobile hangs from one of the sun-drenched court's most striking features—and a marvel of engineering—the immense glass and metal atrium ceiling.

When the East Building officially opened in June 1978, it was an instant hit with the public. Pei's spectacular atrium delighted visitors of all ages. But no feature of his Modernist creation attracted museum-goers more than the knife-edge sharpness of the building's triangular southwest corner. Over the years, the ultra-sharp corner's once pale pink marble has been permanently darkened by the touch of thousands of visitors' hands. Architectural critics also loved the East Building's elegant, triangular geometry and breathtaking central court. Wrote one: "I.M. Pei has produced, in the fullest sense of that hackneyed but unavoidable word, a masterpiece—a structure born of sustained and highly analytical thought, exquisitely attuned to its site and architectural surroundings."

FRANCE'S MOST CHERISHED CULTURAL LANDMARK

The enormous critical and popular success of the East Building brought Pei offers from all over the United States and the world to design other major museums and public buildings. But none was more prestigious—or more challenging—than the commission he received in 1983 from President François Mitterrand of France to expand and modernize the country's

THE PRITZKER ARCHITECTURE PRIZE

In 1983 I.M. Pei was chosen to receive one of the world's most prestigious architecture awards: the Pritzker Architecture Prize. According to the Pritzker Web site, the prize, established in 1979, is awarded each year to honor "living architects whose built work demonstrates a combination of those qualities of talent, vision and commitment, which has produced consistent and significant contributions to humanity and the built environment through the art of architecture." Pei's prize citation declared that "Ieoh Ming Pei has given this century some of its most beautiful interior spaces and exterior forms. Yet the significance of his work goes far beyond that. His concern has always been the surroundings in which his buildings rise." To encourage the development of his profession in his native country, Pei decided to use the $100,000 prize money to fund a scholarship for Chinese architecture students to study in the United States.

famed national art museum and chief cultural and historical landmark, the Louvre.

Located in the heart of Paris, the Louvre was first built as a fortress by the French monarch Philip II in the late 1100s. Nearly four centuries later, King Francis I decided to convert the Louvre into a magnificent royal residence to rival the sumptuous palaces of Renaissance Italy. Over the next 300 years, other French rulers added lavishly decorated rooms, vast courtyards, and two long wings to the palace. By the time construction on the Louvre finally ended, the complex covered nearly 50 acres (20 hectares) and was widely recognized as one of the world's great architectural masterpieces. In 1793, following the French Revolution and the overthrow of King Louis XVI, the Louvre was converted from a royal palace into a public art museum. By the late twentieth century, it housed a half-million works of art

In 1983, I.M. Pei was awarded the Pritzker Architecture Prize, one of the world's leading prizes in the field. Here, he accepts the award at the Metropolitan Museum of Art in New York City.

from Europe and around the globe, including such renowned masterpieces as the Renaissance Italian painter Leonardo da Vinci's *Mona Lisa* and the ancient Greek sculptures *Venus de Milo* and the *Winged Victory of Samothrace.*

Despite the Louvre's stature as one of the world's leading art institutions and France's chief cultural and historical icon, the museum had many serious shortcomings. Essential support facilities such as conservation labs, storage areas, and administrative offices were almost nonexistent. Finding a place to store artwork was a particularly pressing concern for the museum's curators. Because the Louvre's basement lacked humidity or temperature controls, curators were forced to turn over a number of large upstairs rooms to storage. This, combined with the fact that most of one of the palace's three wings had been turned into offices for the French government's Ministry of Finance, left curators with only enough gallery space to display one-tenth of the museum's vast holdings at any given time. Public facilities for guests, such as cafés and information booths, were also in short supply. Even worse, the museum complex was so poorly organized that visitors struggled to find their way through the sprawling museum. "The Louvre was confusing," Cannell observed. "Most of the 3.7 million annual visitors wandered among its labyrinthine corridors in search of three star attractions: the *Venus de Milo*, the *Winged Victory of Samothrace*, and, of course, the *Mona Lisa*. . . . Less prominent treasures required a marathon walk down dingy, unmarked corridors. . . . Too often the Louvre defeated its guests instead of inspiring them."

When Mitterrand first contacted Pei in 1983 about redesigning the Louvre to correct these problems, Pei told the president that he wanted to study the background and layout of the palace complex thoroughly before accepting the commission. Pei did not want to commit himself to Mitterrand's ambitious project, which the French leader had dubbed "Le Grand [Great] Louvre," until he felt confident that there was a way to modernize and enlarge the landmark while also preserving its rich architecture and history. After four months and three lengthy visits to the museum, Pei believed he had found the answer to the dilemma of how to reorganize and expand the Louvre without destroying any of its historic architecture. The new space that the museum so desperately needed, he told Mitterrand, could be found in two places: below the palace complex's gravel-covered central courtyard, the Cour Napoléon, and in the long Richelieu Wing, where the Ministry of Finance had its offices.

Mitterrand immediately agreed to Pei's proposals. He had long ago decided to force the Ministry of Finance out of the Louvre and reclaim the lost gallery space in the Richelieu Wing, anyway. He also realized that digging up the Cour Napoléon, which had become an unsightly parking lot in recent years, and constructing support and visitor facilities beneath the courtyard made perfect sense. For one thing, the vast size of the courtyard meant that there would be more than enough room for the museum's new facilities, including storage and conservation areas, administrative offices, shops, cafeterias, information centers, and a large auditorium. For another, its central location between the U-shaped museum's wings meant that it could serve as the perfect entry point for visitors. According to Pei's plan, once museum-goers descended from the courtyard into the main lobby of the new two-level addition, they would be directed to one of three underground passageways that radiated out from the ticketing area to the Louvre's previously dispersed galleries. As a result of this new organizing scheme, visitors would find getting around the sprawling palace much simpler and less time-consuming than ever before.

THE BATTLE OVER THE PYRAMID

Although many French people would have preferred to have a French architect in charge of redesigning their country's

(continues on page 72)

Between the Generations
CHINESE IMMIGRATION TO AMERICA

The first Chinese immigrants to the United States were drawn by stories of the great California Gold Rush, which began in 1848. Most were young, uneducated men fleeing overpopulation and grinding poverty in their homeland. Many planned to work for a few years as miners or at other menial jobs, then return to China with enough money to buy a small plot of farmland. By 1852, about 25,000 Chinese had made the long ocean voyage to California. As the Western frontier expanded over the next two decades and the demand for cheap labor in the region burgeoned, Chinese immigration to America grew dramatically. Thousands were recruited by the Central Pacific Railroad to lay track for the new transcontinental railway that would link the East and West coasts for the first time. By 1880, more than 100,000 Chinese lived in the United States, the vast majority of them in the Western states.

At first, the Chinese immigrants were welcomed as a useful source of much needed labor. By the 1870s, however, the transcontinental railroad was complete and immigration to the West from other parts of the United States and Europe had exploded. White laborers now found themselves competing for jobs with unemployed Chinese railway workers willing to work for rock-bottom wages. Under the rallying cry, "Chinese must go!," a virulent anti-Chinese movement developed in the West.

In 1882, Congress, bowing to pressure from these anti-Chinese groups, passed the Chinese Exclusion Act, which barred Chinese laborers from immigrating to the United States. (Teachers, students, diplomats, and some merchants were exempted from the law, as were the children of U.S. citizens.) The notorious law made the Chinese the first immigrant group in the United States to be specifically targeted for exclusion. Four decades later, in 1924, Congress passed another blatantly discriminatory law, the National Origins Act, which drastically reduced the number of immigrants allowed into the United States from Eastern and Southern Europe and virtually excluded new immigration from all of Asia.

America's entry into World War II in 1941 proved to be a major turning point for Chinese in the United States. With the Republic of China now a valued ally in the war against Japan, America's anti-Chinese laws had become a national embarrassment. In 1943, Congress passed the Magnuson Act, repealing the Chinese exclusion laws and granting foreign-born Chinese the opportunity to become naturalized U.S. citizens. Nonetheless, the federal government retained strict annual immigration quotas based on national origins, with the yearly quota for Chinese immigrants set at just 105, excepting students and teachers.

Congress finally abolished the quota system with the groundbreaking Immigration and Nationality Act of 1965. After a hiatus of more than eight decades, large-scale Chinese immigration to the United States was able to take place again. In 1960, there were just 237,000 Chinese in the United States. By 2008, an estimated 3.6 million people of Chinese descent lived in the country, making Chinese Americans the largest Asian ethnic group in the United States by a substantial margin. Most immigrants who arrived in the United States during the late twentieth and early twenty-first centuries had little in common with the illiterate and impoverished young men who came to America in the mid-1800s. Women as well as men immigrated, and many were highly educated. They also brought their families with them to the United States, and they came to stay.

Today, Chinese Americans are typically viewed as among the most successful of the various ethnic groups in the United States, with median household incomes and educational levels well above the national average.

(continued from page 69)

beloved cultural icon, they generally supported Pei's inge-nious underground renovation scheme for the Louvre. All that changed in 1984, however, when Pei's blueprint for the aboveground entryway into the museum's new subterranean lobby from the Cour Napoléon was made public. Pei's highly unusual plan for the Louvre's new main entrance was greeted by a firestorm of protest from a shocked French public and press.

Pei's controversial design for the Louvre's new front door was a Modernistic glass pyramid, measuring 116 feet (35 meters) on each side and rising 71 feet (22 meters), about two-thirds of the height of the surrounding palace. Pei wanted to avoid a low, subway-like entrance to the Louvre's new lobby, even though such an entryway would have barely been noticeable at ground level. He thought that the great Louvre deserved a grander entrance than that. Moreover, the glass walls of the pyramid, he reasoned, would provide plenty of natural light for the spacious reception hall below it. In order to illuminate the underground passageways leading from the main lobby to the museum's three wings, Pei also planned to build three smaller glass pyramids flanking the large, central one.

Using a pyramid as opposed to a more conventional struc-ture for the glass-covered entryway, Pei believed, had a num-ber of important advantages. For one, its basic geometric form and clean classic lines meshed well with the Louvre's orderly, symmetrical architecture. For another, a pyramid encloses the largest area within the smallest possible volume of any geometric shape. That meant that a pyramid entrance would provide plenty of space for large numbers of visitors to enter the museum in a short period of time while also being a less distracting presence on the courtyard than a more traditional rectangular building would have been. To make the pyramid virtually transparent and therefore even less likely to divert visitors' attention from the museum's classic architecture, Pei intended to construct it using specially formulated, high-quality glass panes held in place by an ultra-thin system of rods and cables.

Although Mitterrand hailed his architect's unusual design for the entrance as a sparkling "diamond," public opinion in France was overwhelmingly against the pyramid. Newspaper editorials denounced "Pharaoh Pei's pyramid" as a garish

From the entryway in the glass pyramid at the Louvre in Paris, visitors descend into the main lobby for the museum. From there, they can take one of three underground passageways to the Louvre's galleries. With I.M. Pei's plans, the sprawling museum became much easier to navigate.

"atrocity" that would fit better in Disneyland than in the Louvre's elegant and historic courtyard. Ordinary citizens scolded him in the streets of Paris for wanting to disfigure their nation's greatest cultural treasure; Liane Pei even recalled one incensed group of women spitting on her father's feet as he passed by. Although stung by the criticism, Pei refused to change his design. When he is convinced that he is right about something, he once told an interviewer, "I never give up."

With the firm support of Mitterrand and, eventually, the backing of Paris's powerful mayor, Jacques Chirac, as well, Pei managed to get his pyramid entrance built, despite the widespread popular outcry. After the pyramid and Pei's vast underground expansion to the Louvre officially opened in the spring of 1989, something unexpected happened: The French people and press began to warm to the glittering glass and metal structure. By the end of the year, the French newspaper *Le Figaro*, which had mocked Pei's pyramid plan as "absurd" five years earlier, ran a front-page review of the Louvre's new entrance, entitled "The Pyramid Is Very Beautiful After All." Today, two decades after its completion, Pei's world-famous pyramid has become almost as beloved a symbol of Paris as the Eiffel Tower.

In 1993, the second phase of Pei's ambitious project to enlarge the museum, the renovation of the Richelieu Wing, the former headquarters of the Ministry of Finance, was completed. When 165 elegantly redesigned rooms and three sky-lighted sculpture courts totaling more than 200,000 square feet (18,580 square meters) of new exhibition space opened in the refurbished wing that November, the Louvre officially became the world's largest museum. Pei's 10-year-long expansion and modernization of the Louvre won him even greater international acclaim than he had received for the East Building of the National Gallery. Pei considers it his most important and, in the end, also his most satisfying architectural challenge. "The Grand Louvre," he declared, "will hold the first place in my life as an architect."

7

Back to China

In 1974, I.M. Pei returned to his birth country for the first time since he left Shanghai for San Francisco nearly 40 years earlier. After Mao Zedong proclaimed the founding of the Communist People's Republic of China in 1949, the U.S. government cut off all diplomatic ties with China, leaving Pei to wonder if he would ever set foot in his homeland again. Then, in February 1972, President Richard M. Nixon made a historic trip to China to meet with Mao face to face. By the end of Nixon's groundbreaking visit, the Chinese and U.S. governments had agreed to work toward full normalization of diplomatic relations. Two years later, Pei was invited to take part in a cultural exchange tour of China arranged by an American architectural organization. The group of architects visited 11 Chinese cities, including Pei's old hometown, Shanghai. Pei was thrilled to finally have a chance to see China again and reconnect with long-lost relatives and friends.

THE CHINESE GOVERNMENT
MAKES PEI AN OFFER

Pei was both encouraged and saddened by what he found in
the People's Republic of China. When Pei left China in the
mid-1930s, much of the country's huge peasant population was
desperately poor, and hunger and disease were widespread. Pei
thought China's lower classes looked considerably healthier and
better fed after three decades of Communist rule. Yet, while life
had improved for the Chinese peasantry, the country's middle
and upper classes had clearly suffered under Mao's regime. Pei's
immediate family, including his father and siblings, fled China
for Taiwan, Hong Kong, and other parts of Asia after the Communist takeover, but many of his other relatives had remained
behind. As part of their campaign to turn China into a totally
egalitarian society, the Maoists had forced Pei's relations out of
their comfortable homes and put them to work doing manual
labor in factories and warehouses.

During his visit to Shanghai, Pei discovered that some of his
relatives, including his elderly uncle Tsuyuan Pei, had also been
harshly persecuted during the social and political upheaval of
the 1960s and early 1970s known as the Cultural Revolution.
Launched by the Red Guards, a leftist paramilitary group made
up mostly of high school and college students, the Cultural
Revolution was a violent crusade against intellectuals, former
Nationalists, and anyone else whom the radicals suspected of
being insufficiently committed to their hero, Mao Zedong, and
his Communist principles. During the height of the Cultural
Revolution in the late 1960s, Red Guards in Shanghai targeted
Tsuyuan Pei because he had backed Chiang Kai-shek during the
civil war between the Nationalists and the Communists. When
Pei met his uncle in Shanghai, Tsuyuan told him about his
harrowing experiences with the Guards, who had finally been
forced to disband by the Maoist regime several years earlier. The

young fanatics had forced him to take part in humiliating "re-education" sessions and ransacked his apartment, hauling off and destroying cherished family heirlooms including antique paintings, books, porcelain, and even old photos and letters, Tsuyuan confided to his shocked nephew.

In 1978, four years after his eye-opening group tour of China, Pei paid a second visit, this time on his own. The opening of the East Building of the National Gallery that year had turned Pei into an international celebrity, inspiring China's leaders to invite their country's famous native son to Beijing to lecture on architecture and urban planning. By this time, Mao had died and China had a new leader, the reform-minded Deng Xiaoping. Under Deng's moderate and pro-development regime, the People's Republic of China was rapidly modernizing and becoming more accepting of Western culture, which Mao had denounced as corrupting and elitist. (Elitism is the attitude that society should be controlled by a privileged few.) Deng invited Pei to Beijing in 1978 to teach China's leading architects how to design and construct the modern, high-rise office and residential buildings that dominated city skylines in the United States and other Western countries. Pei, however, had no interest in helping Chinese architects build Western-style skyscrapers. Instead, he wanted to inspire them to develop their own modern, yet unmistakably Eastern, style of building.

In his lectures, Pei urged Beijing's architects and urban planners to study their own country's rich cultural traditions rather than slavishly copy Western architectural models. He particularly warned them against erecting skyscrapers near Beijing's chief cultural treasure, the yellow-tiled imperial palace complex known as the Forbidden City. Surrounding the historic complex with towering, Western-style buildings, he argued, would ruin the majestic power of the Forbidden City's vast walled courtyards, from which nothing can be seen except the open sky.

Pei's audiences in Beijing listened politely to what he had to say. But when the Deng regime invited Pei back to the capital for another visit at the end of 1978 to discuss possible design commissions, it was clear that his warnings had fallen on deaf ears. To Pei's dismay, government officials asked him to build a high-rise hotel near the Forbidden City to house the growing numbers of foreign businesspeople and tourists traveling to Beijing. After refusing the commission in the strongest possible terms, Pei managed to talk the officials into formally banning tall buildings within a critical radius of the ancient palace compound. In return, he agreed to take on a different hotel design project for the Chinese government.

FRAGRANT HILL

After looking at a number of possible sites in and near Beijing for the new hotel, Pei settled on a rolling, wooded site about 25 miles (40 kilometers) northwest of the city. Located in a former hunting preserve for China's imperial family called Fragrant Hill, the site was serenely beautiful. Pei thought it would be the ideal location for him to try to develop a modern, yet distinctly Chinese, building style that could serve as a model for China's Western-obsessed architectural community.

Pei began his quest for a new architectural style for his native country by re-examining his own past in the Pei ancestral home of Suzhou. In Suzhou, he discovered that the Communists had turned many of the city's famous walled gardens into public parks. The elegantly landscaped little parks were jam-packed with visitors, which Pei saw as evidence of the continuing importance of gardens in late-twentieth-century Chinese culture. China's enduring love for gardens and nature, he decided, would be the central organizing theme for his modern hotel with a Chinese character.

In his design for the Fragrant Hill Hotel, Pei made nature a priority by building the zigzagging, white-walled resort around

Workers put the finishing touches on a rock sculpture inside the lobby of the Fragrant Hill Hotel in Beijing before its opening in October 1982. The hotel was I.M. Pei's first project in China. He incorporated Chinese traditions into his modern design, but many Chinese officials were disappointed, hoping that the hotel's look would be more Western-oriented.

11 spacious courtyards containing ancient trees, exotic flowers, winding pebble paths, and unusually shaped limestone pillars. Pei had the 20-foot-tall (6-meter-tall) stones specially shipped in from southern China because they reminded him of the natural rock "sculptures" used in Suzhou's ancient gardens. Each of the hotel's 325 guest rooms featured traditional plum-blossom or diamond-shaped windows that provided carefully planned views of the landscaped courtyards below. In traditional Chinese culture, Pei explained to an American interviewer, "windows are not just rectangular openings whose purpose is to let

light in. They are like picture frames in the wall to define exterior views. And the garden is always there."

There could be no mistaking that the Fragrant Hill Hotel was a modern building. Yet its meticulously landscaped courtyards; diamond and blossom-shaped windows; and dramatic "moon gates," large circular openings in garden walls that serve as pedestrian passageways, all evoked China's ancient and distinctive culture, in keeping with Pei's goals for the project. When the Fragrant Hill Hotel was completed in 1982, Pei was pleased with the outcome of his first architectural project in his native country. The less than enthusiastic response that his attempts to incorporate age-old Chinese traditions in his design received from the Western-oriented government officials who had commissioned the hotel, however, dismayed Pei. "The Chinese expressed only tepid enthusiasm for Fragrant Hill; the gulf of understanding was simply too great for them to appreciate what Pei had achieved on their behalf," author Michael Cannell wrote. "I've seen this before," one disappointed Communist official told Pei at the hotel's formal opening. "This looks . . . *Chinese.*"

THE BANK OF CHINA, HONG KONG

Despite their disappointment with what they considered his overly traditional approach to Fragrant Hill, the Deng regime asked Pei to design another building shortly after the hotel's completion. They wanted Pei to design the new Hong Kong branch of the Bank of China (BOC), which at that time was totally owned by the Chinese government. The government had decided to open a Hong Kong office in 1982, when Great Britain agreed to hand over its longtime colony to the People's Republic of China, with the formal transfer scheduled for 1997. The Communists were eager to hire an internationally

(continues on page 84)

Being Asian American | AN AMERICAN ARCHITECT'S CHINESE ROOTS

Although I.M. Pei has lived in the United States since he was 18 years old, his Chinese cultural heritage remains an important factor in his approach to architecture. "I have two worlds," he once said. "It is difficult for me to practice architecture without occasionally looking back into my own background."

According to Pei, his frequent childhood visits to the family garden, Shizilin or Forest of Stone Lions, near his grandfather's house in Suzhou, were particularly critical in shaping his attitudes toward the art and practice of building. In common with most of Suzhou's other famous walled gardens, the Forest of Stone Lions was decorated with unusually shaped limestone "sculptures." The large stones had been deliberately eroded over periods of many years and gathered from nearby lakes and rivers by so-called rock farmers. Pei explained the influence that the traditional Chinese gardens of his childhood and their unique, weathered artwork had on his development as an architect in an interview with the *Christian Science Monitor* more than four decades after he left his homeland for America. In the interview, when Pei used the word *metaphysical*, he meant of or relating to an order of existence beyond that which people can discover with their five senses. "In China, rocks were traditionally endowed with metaphysical importance. They were valued for distinct spirits—the cosmic vapors—inhabiting their forms," Pei's biographer, Michael Cannell, observed. Regarding the ancient rock gardens of Suzhou and the men who helped create them, Pei told the *Christian Science Monitor:*

> How such gardens are made, or I should say harvested, is very interesting. You see, these rock farmers were and are artists—and you can go beyond the gardens to the whole environment of Suzhou . . . all of it has instilled a lasting metaphysical image, if not a direct influence, on the shape of my

work. The way those rock farmers did things pertains to a perception of time, and to a sense of accountability to time.

They usually worked with a porous volcanic rock, and they selected the rocks most carefully. Then they chiseled them most carefully, just enough to open up that piece of rock to the subtle sculptural spirit that the particular farmer wanted—yet the rock would still be very raw, not unlike the perforations and imperfections implanted by time when the farmer found it. Then he would find, almost carefully, a spot near the edge of a lake or a stream. And he would place the rock, just so, into the water, which, over a generation, or sometimes over two or three, would erode the shape. The farmer himself, or his son or grandson, would later harvest the shape, incorporating it into the composition of the garden.

This sense of connection, of continuity, is an extremely telling aspect of Chinese culture—the father will sow, the son will reap—and, in principle, it is a primary impulse in considering the results of any action.

... My own development, when I stop to think about it, is very much in that spirit. I have been placed at the edge, or often at the center, of many different lakes and streams. And my buildings, like those of every architect, are always being pulled out of the flow of the water and put back in. Their shapes have hopefully been chosen most carefully, placed most carefully to respond to the functional currents swirling around them. ... An architect has to try (and I have tried) to participate in such a way that his buildings become congenial, caring, and cared-for expressions of that flow. It took me a while to understand this dimension of design—to design in the spirit of that garden of my childhood. And once you build in that spirit—how it humbles you.

(continued from page 81)

renowned architect like Pei because they viewed the new bank building as an important symbol of China's growing financial power. Pei decided to accept the commission for two reasons. First, he believed that the project represented "the aspirations of the Chinese people," as the country was finally emerging from more than a quarter of a century of economic isolation and backwardness under Mao Zedong. His second reason for taking the commission was more personal. He saw the project as a tribute to his 89-year-old father, who had spent nearly three-and-a-half decades as a manager for the Bank of China before Mao took power.

Pei faced a number of challenges in designing the bank's new Hong Kong office, beginning with the small size of the site, which meant that the building would have to be very tall to have the amount of office space the Chinese government wanted. Yet, because Hong Kong is subject to violent tropical cyclones known as typhoons, the 70-story structure would have to be strong enough to withstand winds of more than 100 miles per hour (161 kilometers per hour). Pei's imaginative solution to the problem of constructing a very tall building that could resist typhoon-force gales involved a unique, asymmetrical tower made up of four triangular shafts sheathed in silver-coated reflective glass. As Pei's shimmering tower rises into the sky, the shafts gradually become narrower and narrower, much like "a sprouting bamboo that propels its stalk successively higher with each new growth," author Judith Dupré wrote. The triangular shafts are not only strikingly attractive, but also highly functional, since they transfer the weight of the entire building onto four huge steel corner columns and one central column. As a result of this simple yet highly effective design, the Bank of China Tower required significantly less steel to construct than more traditional rectangular skyscrapers, yet it is still strong enough to stand up to extreme winds.

I.M. Pei's Bank of China Tower *(left)*, which opened in 1989, stands next to the Cheung Kong Centre tower in Hong Kong. Pei's asymmetrical tower consists of four triangular shafts that gradually become narrower. His design allowed for a tall building that could withstand winds from the typhoons that strike Hong Kong.

Almost universally admired by architectural critics and structural engineers as well as by the Chinese officials who commissioned the project, the Bank of China Tower had the distinction of being the tallest building outside of the United States when it opened in 1989. The project ended up being a bittersweet experience for Pei, however. Throughout construction, he was forced to deal with angry complaints from local feng shui experts, who blasted almost every aspect of his design as promoting "bad energy," from the two tall broadcast masts on its rooftop to the placement of its main entryway. An ancient Chinese concept, feng shui teaches that people can use the laws of earth and heaven to achieve harmony among the natural energies of any given space, thereby promoting happiness, prosperity, and health. Architects who choose to ignore these universal laws, as Pei was accused of doing in his bank design, supposedly create negative energy, bringing bad fortune not only to those who work or live in their buildings, but also to the neighboring community.

Adding to the bittersweet nature of the project was a shocking event that occurred in Beijing as the tower was nearing completion in 1989. In early June, government troops killed more than 1,000 unarmed pro-democracy protesters, most of them college students, on Tiananmen Square in Beijing. Pei, who had taken the Bank of China project in part to show his support for the more moderate and open direction that China had taken since Deng Xiaoping took power, felt personally betrayed by the regime's violent actions against the demonstrators. After the bank building officially opened just three months later, Pei decided to focus his attention on architectural projects outside of his birth country for the time being. During the decade ahead, an exciting and remarkably diverse group of commissions would take Pei from the shores of Lake Erie in bustling Cleveland, Ohio, to a remote valley in the mountains above Kyoto, Japan.

8

A Busy "Retirement"

In 1990, I.M. Pei officially retired from the architectural firm he had founded in New York City 35 years earlier. At age 73, Pei was not ready to give up designing buildings, by any means. But he was more than ready to hand over the day-to-day responsibilities of running an architectural organization of 300 employees to his two senior partners, Henry Cobb and James Ingo Freed. For the first time in his long architectural career, he also wanted to have complete freedom in deciding which design commissions to accept or decline, without feeling obliged to make "the bottom line" (in other words, financial profit) a top priority. Before he could concentrate all of his attention on independent projects, however, Pei had one big commission left from his days as senior partner at Pei, Cobb, Freed & Partners to complete: the Rock and Roll Hall of Fame and Museum in Cleveland, Ohio.

THE ROCK AND ROLL HALL OF FAME

In 1987, the project's two leading sponsors, magazine publisher Jann Wenner and music executive Ahmet Ertegun of the Rock and Roll Hall of Fame Foundation, had asked Pei to design a permanent home for their organization in Cleveland, Ohio. The Rock and Roll Hall of Fame Foundation's chief aim was to honor the contributions of musicians who had significantly shaped the development and evolution of rock and roll. Besides housing the Hall of Fame, the foundation's new building was also to serve as a museum of the history of rock and roll. The foundation's officers had chosen Cleveland as the site for the hall of fame and museum in recognition of the fact that a Cleveland disc jockey, Alan Freed, had first coined the term *rock 'n' roll* in the early 1950s. Political and business leaders in Cleveland were enthusiastic about the project, which they hoped would help revitalize the city's decaying downtown.

At first, Pei was reluctant to accept Wenner and Ertegun's offer. "When the committee from the Rock and Roll Hall of Fame Foundation came and asked me to design the building, I was taken aback," Pei later confided to an interviewer. "I told them, 'You know, I'm not a fan. I'm really not.' When I thought of rock and roll, all I thought of was my kids, and with me it was always, 'Kids, turn it down. Turn it *down.*'" But after Wenner and Ertegun promised to give Pei a crash course in rock music, including a guided tour of the late Elvis Presley's Graceland Mansion in Memphis, Tennessee, he agreed to take the commission. Pei's children, all of whom were now adults, were both surprised and delighted by his decision.

Pei wanted his design for the Rock and Roll Hall of Fame and Museum to reflect what he saw as the music's two essential qualities: "tremendous youthful energy" and "rebellion." Pei's attempt to translate rock's rebellious spirit and explosive energy into his Hall of Fame design began with a pyramid-like, central glass and steel atrium from which all the other wings "seem to blast outward . . . like a fleet of spaceships," Robert Campbell, architectural critic for *The Boston Globe*, observed after the building opened in 1995. In addition to a six-story rectangular

Thousands of people flocked to the grand opening of the Rock and Roll Hall of Fame and Museum in Cleveland, Ohio, in September 1995. Critics gave mixed reviews to I.M. Pei's design, wondering if the architect had connected with the project. "It looks like a Pei building, but it doesn't feel like one," one critic wrote.

tower containing 50,000 square feet (4,645 square meters) of exhibition space, the structure includes a 175-seat auditorium cantilevered (extended outward) over Lake Erie on one side of the glass atrium or "tent," as Pei dubbed the museum's soaring entryway. On the opposite side of the atrium, a circular drum perches atop a slender concrete column rising from the water. Like the rest of the structure except for the central "tent," the exterior walls of this striking theater-in-the-round are sheathed in gleaming white metal panels.

When the Rock and Roll Hall of Fame and Museum officially opened in September 1995, Pei's building, although a huge hit with the public, received mixed reviews from architectural critics. Many of them doubted that Pei had ever truly become emotionally engaged in the project. Carter Wiseman, a respected architectural critic as well as Pei's biographer, wrote that:

> The building lacked a sense of architectural enthusiasm. The dramatic geometric shapes, the soaring atrium, the crisscrossing escalators, all bespoke a Pei building, but the fundamental lack of cultural sympathy among architect, program, and client had caught up with Pei's

THE MORTON H. MEYERSON SYMPHONY CENTER

In 1989, the same year that the Bank of China Tower opened in Hong Kong and one year before Pei announced his retirement from Pei, Cobb, Freed & Partners, one of Pei's most spectacular and admired buildings opened in Dallas, Texas: the Morton H. Meyerson Symphony Center. Pei's first concert hall is a limestone rectangle surrounded by dramatic curves of glass. Funded by a group of Texas oil magnates, the building cost more than $80 million. At the time of its completion in September 1989, Pei described his stunningly modern creation in his published "Architect's Statement" for the project:

> The plan of the Morton H. Meyerson Symphony Center is a combination of overlapping geometric forms. It starts with a rectangle set at an angle within a square and is enveloped by segments of circles. The central rectangular form houses the performance hall. Surrounding it, under a sweeping glass canopy, are various layers of . . . public space, including an expansive skylit lobby . . . and sculpture garden. . . .
>
> The building program required a design that would accommodate two different, but related, functions. Of

best intentions and dampened any spark from the original inspiration. ... It looks like a Pei building, but it doesn't feel like one.

A decade after the Hall of Fame was completed, Pei himself admitted: "I have more confidence about other buildings than I do about this one. I came at it the best way I could based on what I was able to learn at the time. I'm much older now, and farther away from rock and roll, but I think I might do it better."

paramount importance is the performance hall. Its forms and shape are the result of rigorous adherence to the acoustician's requirements for audience distribution, unobstructed sight lines, and acoustical excellence. Seating 2,062 people on four levels, the concert hall focuses on the performance platform and on the grand concert organ. Suspended above the orchestra is a back-lit acoustical canopy which ... can be mechanically raised or lowered for perfected symphonic sound. Notwithstanding technical constrains, the hall was designed to possess a quality of ambience that gives pleasure to the making of, and the listening to, music.

In contrast to the necessarily closed character of the performance hall, the surrounding public areas are transparent by day and night, offering an inviting place to congregate when performances are not in progress. These intricately glazed spaces have been designed to provide visual excitement through the manipulation of light, movement, and changing perspectives. In this way, the Meyerson Symphony Center reaches out to a larger public than those attending performances.

"THE JOY OF ANGELS"

The first commission that Pei accepted after deciding to retire from his firm was different from anything he had ever tried before. His client for the project, Mihoko Koyama, was the elderly leader of a Japanese religious sect called Shinji Shumei-kai. Founded in 1970 by Mrs. Koyama, Shinji Shumeikai stresses the role of beauty in art and nature in bringing a sense of spiritual meaning and joy to people's lives. When Mrs. Koyama first approached Pei regarding the commission in 1988, while he was still with Pei, Cobb, Freed & Partners, Pei turned her down. The project, a bell tower to be erected near the sect's main temple in rural Shigo, Japan, was too small and specialized for the firm to take on, he explained. He did promise, however, to visit Mrs. Koyama and her daughter Hiroko on his next trip to Asia to see the tower site in person and talk with them more about the project.

When Pei finally made it to Shigo nearly a year after meeting Mrs. Koyama at his New York City office, he had already set a firm retirement date of January 1990 and was prepared to reconsider her offer as a personal project. After seeing the serenely beautiful site in the mountainous terrain outside of Kyoto where the bell tower was to be built, Pei knew at once that he wanted the commission. Pei then had what he would describe as an almost otherworldly experience. Thinking about the form that the bell tower should take, he suddenly remembered an elegantly shaped Japanese *bachi* he had bought on a trip to Kyoto with his wife many years earlier. A bachi is a small, flat plectrum, or pick, used to pluck the strings of traditional Japanese musical instruments like the three-stringed *shamisen*. Bachis come in many shapes, but Pei's bachi had a particularly appealing form, with a slender base that flared gracefully outward at the top. Regarding his unusual selection of a model for the bell tower, Pei later said: "My decision was not rational, except to the extent that the bachi and the tower both have a musical function. It was a choice I would almost qualify as mystic." To sheath the exterior of the 197-foot-high (60-meter-high) tower, he wanted white granite imported from Vermont because he thought the local stone his client had selected was too dark. Mrs. Koyama, who was the heiress to a huge Japanese textile fortune and one of the richest women in Asia, immediately agreed to Pei's suggestion, although shipping the heavy granite from the United States to the Shigo site would add an extra $1 million to the project's final cost.

When the Shinji Shumeikai bell tower was completed in 1990, Mrs. Koyama named it "The Joy of Angels" in honor of an ancient picture she had seen in a Kyoto temple of an angel with a bachi. Although much smaller in scale than any of his previous projects, the bell tower proved an immensely satisfying project for Pei. As Michael Cannell observed, "It was the closest Pei ever came to pure sculpture." According to Carter Wiseman, Pei was also drawn to the project's spiritual aspect. "Even though I didn't know much about the religion," Pei said, "it was a challenge to try to capture its spirit. It was a search for the sort of expression that is not at all technical."

A JAPANESE SHANGRI-LA

Mrs. Koyama and her daughter Hiroko were so pleased with how "The Joy of Angels" bell tower turned out that they quickly offered Pei another commission. For years, Mrs. Koyama had been collecting historic Japanese tea ceremony objects, which she now wanted to share with the public. She asked Pei to build a small museum to display the collection not far from the bell tower. Pei was enthusiastic about designing another art museum, particularly one in such a spectacular natural setting. But he had two concerns about the project. First, he doubted that Mrs. Koyama's relatively small collection of tea ceremony utensils would attract many visitors to her museum, given that it would be a 20-mile (32-kilometer) drive from the closest city, Kyoto. On Pei's advice, Mrs. Koyama decided to expand and diversify the museum's collection to include historic artworks and other objects connected to the Silk Road. (The Silk Road was the ancient overland trade route between China and the Mediterranean world that linked Asia with Europe and North Africa.) Pei's second concern was the site she and her daughter had selected for the museum. Located at the bottom of a deep valley, the site was too close to the temple's main parking lot, Pei believed. When the Koyamas came up with a second site high on a mountain slope overlooking the valley, however, Pei immediately agreed to accept the commission.

The new museum's isolated mountainous site created a number of challenges for Pei, but the biggest one was how to get visitors to it. Local consultants suggested cutting a road through the mountainous terrain leading to the site. Pei, however, wanted an approach to the building that would preserve as much of the landscape as possible while also providing a sense of drama and mystery to the museum. For inspiration, he turned to a classic Chinese fable by the fourth-century poet and scholar Tao Yuan Ming entitled "Peach Blossom Spring," which he had loved as a child. In the story, a fisherman exploring a mountain stream suddenly stumbles on a landscape of unearthly beauty that has remained untouched by time, like the mythical Shangri-La described in British author James Hilton's famous twentieth-century novel, *Lost Horizon*. As it turned out, Mrs. Koyama, like many highly educated Japanese of her era, was familiar with classic Chinese literature, and she, too, had enjoyed "Peach Blossom Spring" as a child. With her enthusiastic backing, Pei decided to design the approach to the museum so that visitors would come upon the building and its pristine mountainside site suddenly, just as the Chinese fisherman in the ancient story had unexpectedly come upon his Shangri-La.

The Miho Museum, which opened in 1997, is on a secluded mountain site outside of Kyoto, Japan. I.M. Pei wanted to create an element of surprise in getting to the museum. Visitors first see the building after emerging through a tunnel.

To give museum visitors the sensation of having stumbled upon a hidden paradise when they first saw the building, Pei had a 656-foot (200-meter) steel-lined tunnel dug through a neighboring mountain. Connected to the tunnel is an artfully designed suspension bridge that almost seems to float above the intervening valley below. As visitors emerge from the tunnel onto the bridge, they get their first tantalizing glimpse of the museum's slanted glass roofs rising above the tree-covered mountain slope. To help the building blend in with its surroundings and at the same time preserve the museum's natural environment, Pei placed nearly 80 percent of the 99,469-square-foot (9,241-square-meter) museum underground. To give his

Modernistic design for the building a Japanese spirit, he linked the paved plaza at the foot of the museum to the entrance hall with terraced steps like those of a traditional Japanese temple. The museum's sharply slanted rooflines also deliberately echoed the sloped roofs of Japan's ancient religious shrines.

After completing the Miho Museum, which officially opened to the public in 1997, Pei continued to focus on international projects, designing the Grand-Duc Jean Museum of Modern Art in Luxembourg and an addition to the German Historical Museum in Berlin. Then, soon after the turn of the new century, the 84-year-old architect began work on a challenging new project that was particularly close to his heart: a Modernistic museum with a Chinese spirit in the historic center of his family's ancestral home: Suzhou.

9

Into the Twenty-First Century

Designing and building the Suzhou Museum was truly a family affair for I.M. Pei. The acclaimed art museum, which opened in the Pei ancestral home of Suzhou, China, in 2006, was the product not only of I.M.'s expertise and efforts, but also those of his sons: T'ing Pei, an urban planner, and architects Chien Chung (Didi) and Li Chung Pei (Sandi).

Pei's eldest child, T'ing, was the first of his three sons to become involved in the Suzhou project. T'ing's connection with it began in the mid-1990s, after Suzhou's mayor asked I.M. Pei to design a new building for the Suzhou Museum. The museum's valuable collection of paintings, calligraphy, and porcelain from the Ming (1368–1644) and Qing (1644–1911) dynasties had outgrown its current home in a historic mansion in the heart of Suzhou. Pei loved the idea of designing a major cultural institution for his family's hometown. Nonetheless, he refused to consider the mayor's request until Suzhou's government developed a detailed plan to preserve the city's historic sections in the face of rapid economic and population growth and clean up

I.M. Pei worked with his three sons in developing the plans for the Suzhou Museum in Pei's ancestral hometown. Officials in Suzhou wanted the museum, which opened in 2006, to be a modern facility yet still reflect the Chinese city's traditional building style.

its badly polluted canals. On I.M.'s recommendation, T'ing and the American architecture and environment consulting company EDAW held a two-week workshop in 1996 in Suzhou with local urban planners and architects to examine how to improve the city's water quality, protect its rich historical and cultural heritage, and modernize its housing. Five years later, with the Suzhou government making solid progress toward achieving these goals, Pei agreed to design the new museum in collaboration with Pei Partnership Architects, Didi and Sandi's firm. Didi and Sandi Pei had founded their architectural partnership in 1992 after spending the first two decades of their careers working for their father on such projects as the Louvre expansion and the Bank of China Tower in Hong Kong. Since its establishment, Pei Partnership had been awarded many commissions in Asia, including the Bank of China's new headquarters in Beijing, which opened in 2001 and included a spectacular sky-lit atrium co-designed by I.M. Pei.

SUZHOU MUSEUM

The Suzhou Museum presented many challenges for Pei. The museum site was located deep within Suzhou's oldest district, across from a historic palace and backed against one of the largest of the city's famous walled gardens, the sixteenth-century Garden of the Humble Administrator. City officials wanted the museum to be a twenty-first-century facility. Yet they insisted that the new structure reflect Suzhou's traditional building style. Although the new building needed to be large enough to house a 30,000-piece art collection, its height could not exceed 52.5 feet (16 meters), in order to harmonize with its historic neighbors. Pei was also informed that the walls, roof, and exterior trim of the museum had to be constructed from Suzhou's customary building materials of plaster, stone, or tile in the city's traditional colors of gray and white.

Pei spent many months toiling over a design that was respectful of Suzhou's architectural traditions while also pointing toward the rapidly developing city's future. In the end, his design incorporated the whitewashed plaster walls typical of Suzhou's historic buildings but not their customary upturned, gray tile roofs. Instead, Pei decided to use a blue-gray granite to cover the roofs of the sharply angled museum, cap its walls, and outline its unusual hexagonal and diamond-shaped windows. The overall effect of the sprawling, 183,000-square-foot (17,000-square-meter) museum, noted writer Robert Ivy, is "decidedly modern" yet with a distinctly Chinese spirit.

In keeping with Suzhou's cultural traditions, Pei placed a large, walled garden at the center of the museum complex.

PEI'S MOST CHERISHED HONOR

Since the beginning of his architectural career in the 1940s, I.M. Pei has received dozens of prestigious awards. They include the Gold Medal of the American Institute of Architects, the Pritzker Architecture Prize, the Grande Médaille d'Or from France's Académie d'Architecture, and the Japan Art Association's Praemium Imperiale for lifetime achievement in architecture. In 1992, President George H.W. Bush awarded Pei the Presidential Medal of Freedom, the highest civilian award in the United States, for his "especially meritorious contribution to . . . cultural or other significant public or private endeavors." Yet, no medal or award that he has received over the years has been more important to Pei than the Medal of Liberty, presented to him in 1986 by President Ronald Reagan.

The Medal of Liberty was specially created to commemorate the 100th anniversary of the Statue of Liberty. It was awarded on July 4, 1986, to Pei and 11 other foreign-born U.S. citizens for their outstanding contributions to American life. After the awards ceremony, Pei was asked what the medal meant to him. According to author Carter Wiseman, Pei answered "that while he had never suffered from racial discrimination in the United States, he had, at least in the early days, sometimes felt like 'an outsider.' Even though he has been an American citizen since 1955, . . . his eyes suddenly grew moist as he described how important the medal was to him as a symbol that he had been accepted by the American people."

He made sure that the spacious garden could be easily seen from the museum's galleries and passageways as well as its big entry hall. In traditional Chinese architecture, he explained, "garden and building are one—they are not separate. . . . There is no distinction between garden and rooms; they are joined together." Pei decorated the museum gardens with such classically Chinese features as a lotus pool crossed by a graceful footbridge, a tea pavilion, a bamboo grove, and a dramatic, natural rock sculpture. I.M., Didi, and Sandi selected and arranged every tree, shrub, and rock used in the courtyards, paying especially close attention to the granite boulders that made up the rock sculpture. Rather than try to imitate the oddly shaped, weathered limestone sculptures of Suzhou's ancient walled gardens, Pei decided to have thinly sliced granite slabs shipped to the site from

(continues on page 104)

I.M. Pei has said that the most important honor he has received was the Medal of Liberty in 1986. Here, he accepts the award from President Ronald Reagan and first lady Nancy Reagan. The medal, commemorating the 100th anniversary of the Statue of Liberty, was presented to 12 foreign-born U.S. citizens.

Other Notable Individuals

MAYA LIN

Maya Lin was born on October 5, 1959, in Athens, Ohio. Her parents, Julia Chang of Shanghai and Henry Huan Lin of Beijing, immigrated separately to the United States from China shortly before Mao Zedong's Red Army defeated the Nationalist forces of Chiang Kai-shek in 1949. Both came from well-to-do families with ties to the Nationalists, and both feared they would face persecution under Mao's Communist regime. Julia Lin, who was smuggled out of Shanghai on a fishing boat after the city fell to the Red Army in May 1949, attended Smith College in Massachusetts and went on to teach Asian and English literature at Ohio University. Henry Lin, a skilled ceramist, was a dean of fine arts at Ohio University.

After graduating from high school at the top of her class, Maya Lin attended Yale University in New Haven, Connecticut, where she studied architecture and sculpture. In 1981, while she was a senior at Yale, Lin entered a nationwide competition to create a design for the Vietnam Veterans Memorial in Washington, D.C. That May, the 21-year-old Chinese American became an instant celebrity when a panel of artists and architects selected her design from more than 1,400 entries. Lin's simple memorial featured a V-shaped, highly polished black granite wall engraved with the names of the more than 58,000 Americans who died or were unaccounted for in the Vietnam War (1959–1975). Because Lin's stark design was very different from traditional war monuments, which typically featured patriotic inscriptions and heroic-size statues, it created a great deal of controversy at first. After the memorial was completed in 1982, however, Lin's somber and moving tribute to the fallen and missing U.S. servicemen and servicewomen quickly became one of the most admired and visited sites in the national capital.

After earning her bachelor of art degree from Yale in 1981, Lin briefly enrolled in a graduate program in architecture at Harvard University and then worked for two years for an architectural firm in Boston. She returned to Yale in 1984 and completed the requirements for a master of architecture degree in 1986. In 1988, Lin was asked by the Southern Poverty Law Center in Montgomery, Alabama, to design a memorial to Americans who lost their lives in support of the civil-rights movement from the early 1950s until the assassination of Dr. Martin Luther King, Jr., in April 1968. The project was destined to become her most widely acclaimed work after the Vietnam Veterans Memorial. Lin's striking design is made up of two parts. The first is a 12-foot-diameter (3.7-meter-diameter) black granite disk inscribed with the names of 40 fallen heroes of the civil-rights movement and 21 landmark dates in their struggle for racial equality. The second is a circular black granite wall engraved with a quotation from Dr. King's famous "I Have a Dream" speech of 1963 at the Lincoln Memorial in Washington, D.C: "Until justice rolls down like waters and righteousness like a mighty stream." Water cascades over the polished stone of both parts of the memorial, which was formally dedicated in November 1989.

During her nearly three-decade career, Lin has won many prestigious honors and prizes for her work, including the Award in Architecture from the American Academy of Arts and Letters and the Presidential Design Award. Her diverse art and architectural projects include the Langston Hughes Library in Clinton, Tennessee; the Women's Table at Yale University; a landscape sculpture, *The Wave Field*, at the University of Michigan in Ann Arbor; and, most recently, the Confluence Project. The Confluence Project consists of seven outdoor installations along the Columbia River system in the Pacific Northwest that interweave the history of the nineteenth-century explorers Lewis and Clark with the experiences of the Native American tribes they came in contact with along their way. Lin's most recent project is the new building for the Museum of Chinese in America in New York City's Chinatown, which opened in the summer of 2009. The museum includes a landscaped courtyard that Lin says is patterned on the central courtyard in her mother's childhood home in Shanghai.

(continued from page 101)

northern China. Inspired by a Song Dynasty (960–1279) scroll depicting overlapping mountains, Pei personally directed workmen as they used a crane to arrange the 10-ton slices in various positions against a garden wall until the rocks resembled a sort of three-dimensional version of the ancient scroll painting.

THE MUSEUM OF ISLAMIC ART

When the Suzhou Museum opened to the public in 2006, Pei told an interviewer that he hoped the building would encourage a new type of architecture in China, one that was modern yet at the same time honored the country's ancient cultural heritage. In another major architectural project that Pei tackled after the turn of the twenty-first century, the Museum of Islamic Art in Doha, Qatar, he also sought to link the present with the past. In his widely praised design for the Middle Eastern museum, which was completed in late 2008, Pei skillfully blended modern elements with elements from traditional Islamic architecture.

The emir (ruler) of Qatar wanted his state's new museum to display historic Islamic artwork from all over the world, including Spain and India, both of which were once important centers of Islamic civilization, as well as the Middle East. Inspired by the diversity of the collection that the emir was attempting to assemble, after accepting the museum commission, Pei spent months visiting traditional Muslim buildings on three continents in search of what he called "the essence of Islamic architecture." He finally discovered what he was looking for in a covered ablution fountain at the Ibn Tulun Mosque in Cairo, Egypt. (Muslims use ablution fountains for ritual cleansing before entering a mosque for prayer.) Dating from the 800s, the high-domed, stone structure has a simple, strongly geometric

According to I.M. Pei, the Museum of Islamic Art in Doha, Qatar, which opened in November 2008, is the last large-scale project that he will design. As with many of his previous architectural gems, the museum links the present with the past, combining contemporary design with traditional Islamic elements.

form that "comes to life in the sun, with its shadows and shades of color," Pei observed.

Located on a specially constructed artificial island in the Persian Gulf about 200 feet (60 meters) from shore, the Museum of Islamic Art is as severely geometric in form as the ancient Ibn Tulun fountain or as a modern sculpture. Pei's contemporary yet clearly Islamic-influenced design is a "bridge between modernity and tradition" and "past and present," observes the museum's curator, Sabiha Al-Khemir. Pei's many references to traditional Islamic culture in the museum's Modernistic interior include an enormous ring-shaped lamp that hangs below the central atrium's stainless steel dome and is similar to the hanging lamps found in some historic mosques. At the institution's formal opening in November 2008, Pei, who admitted to knowing little about Islamic civilization when he first accepted the commission seven years earlier, told a journalist that the museum "is very special to me. It helped me learn something, not just about building but about culture."

Shortly before the Museum of Islamic Art was completed, Pei revealed that Qatar's new cultural institution would be his final large-scale project. As of the spring of 2009, the 92-year-old architect is still actively engaged in designing buildings, however. Reportedly, his latest commission is a small chapel outside Kyoto, Japan. In a recent interview, Pei said about his chosen profession: "Architecture is stones and brick, concrete and steel. Architecture has to endure." In a career that has spanned nearly seven decades, I.M. Pei has left the world an architectural legacy of remarkable grace, originality, and scope that will surely continue to endure and inspire for many years to come.

CHRONOLOGY

1917 Born on April 26 in Guangzhou, China.

1918 Pei family moves to the British colony of Hong Kong.

1927 Pei family moves to Shanghai, China.

1930 Pei's mother, Lien Kwun, dies.

1935 Travels to the United States to attend college.

1940 Earns bachelor of architecture degree from the Massachusetts Institute of Technology.

1942 Marries Eileen Loo.

1943–1945 Serves on U.S. National Defense Research Committee.

1946 Earns master of architecture degree from Harvard University.

1948 Hired as director of architectural research for real estate developer William Zeckendorf.

1952 Begins work on the Mile High Center in Denver.

1955 Becomes a naturalized U.S. citizen. Founds architectural partnership of I.M. Pei & Associates.

1961 Begins to design the National Center for Atmospheric Research near Boulder, Colorado.

1964 Jacqueline Kennedy chooses Pei to design the John F. Kennedy Presidential Library.

1978 National Gallery of Art, East Building, opens in Washington, D.C.

1979 John F. Kennedy Presidential Library opens.

1982 Fragrant Hill Hotel in Beijing opens.
1983 Awarded the Pritzker Architecture
Prize.
1986 Awarded the Medal of Liberty.
1989 The Louvre glass-pyramid expansion opens
in Paris; The Bank of China Tower opens in
Hong Kong.
1992 Receives the Presidential Medal
of Freedom.

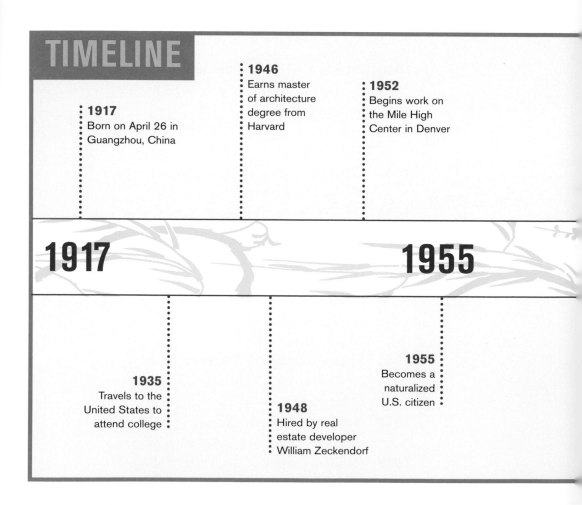

TIMELINE

1946
Earns master
of architecture
degree from
Harvard

1952
Begins work on
the Mile High
Center in Denver

1917
Born on April 26 in
Guangzhou, China

1917

1955

1935
Travels to the
United States to
attend college

1948
Hired by real
estate developer
William Zeckendorf

1955
Becomes a
naturalized
U.S. citizen

1993 Second phase of the Louvre expansion opens.

1995 Rock and Roll Hall of Fame and Museum opens in Cleveland.

1997 Miho Museum opens in Shiga, Japan.

2006 Suzhou Museum opens in Suzhou, China.

2008 Museum of Islamic Art opens in Doha, Qatar.

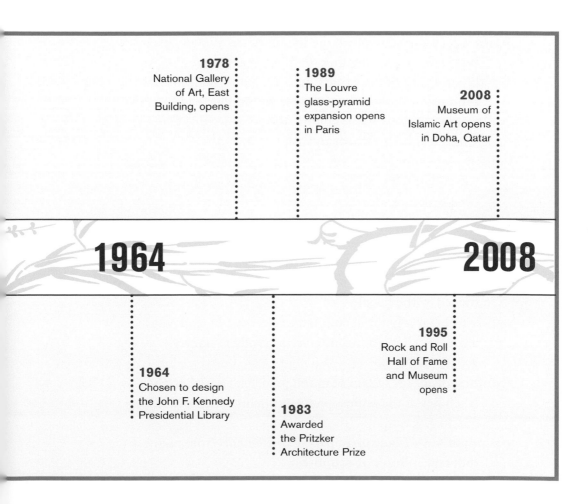

1978
National Gallery of Art, East Building, opens

1989
The Louvre glass-pyramid expansion opens in Paris

2008
Museum of Islamic Art opens in Doha, Qatar

1964   **2008**

1964
Chosen to design the John F. Kennedy Presidential Library

1983
Awarded the Pritzker Architecture Prize

1995
Rock and Roll Hall of Fame and Museum opens

GLOSSARY

ablution fountain—In Islamic tradition, an ablution fountain is used for ritual cleansing before a worshipper enters a mosque for prayer.

architecture —The science and art of designing and constructing buildings.

atrium—A many-storied and usually sky-lighted central area in a building.

bachi—A pick used to pluck the strings of traditional Japanese instruments like the three-stringed shamisen.

Buddhism—One of the world's great religions, Buddhism was founded in India in the 500s B.C. by Siddhartha Gautama.

calligraphy—In East Asian culture, the art of writing Chinese characters with a brush and ink.

cast-in-place concrete—Concrete cast or molded in a form at the building site before being placed into its final position on a structure.

catwalk—A narrow, elevated walkway.

Communism—An economic and social system in which private property no longer exists and all of a country's resources and means of production are communally owned by the people.

concession—A territorial concession is a tract of land within a country that is administered by another country's government.

Confucianism—A system of moral principles based on the teachings of the philosopher Confucius, who lived from 551 to 479 B.C.

cosmopolitan—Made up of people or elements from many different cultures or countries.

façade—The face of a building.

feng shui—An ancient Chinese concept based on the belief that people can use the laws of earth and heaven to achieve harmony among the natural energies of any given space, thereby promoting happiness, health, and prosperity.

landscape architecture—The arrangement of land, together with the buildings and other objects on it, for human use and enjoyment.

mesa—Commonly found in the Southwestern United States, a mesa is a flat, elevated area with one or more cliff-like sides.

Modernist architecture—Rooted in the early twentieth century, Modernist architecture, like the International Movement that grew out of it, sought to break with the styles and techniques of the past to create a new type of architecture that reflected the spirit of the modern, industrial age.

moon gate—In traditional Chinese architecture, a moon gate is a large, circular opening in a garden wall that serves as a pedestrian passageway.

neoclassical architecture—Neoclassical architecture is inspired by the classical architecture of ancient Greece and Rome.

opium—An addictive narcotic drug extracted from the seedpods of the opium poppy plant.

philanthropist—Someone who tries to better the well-being of other people, usually through donations or charitable aid.

portico—A columned porch or walkway that generally leads to the entrance of a building.

pyramid—A structure with a square base and four triangular sides that join at a point.

quarry—An open pit from which stones are extracted by cutting, digging, or blasting.

Silk Road—The ancient trade route between China and the Mediterranean world that linked the Far East with Europe and North Africa.

typhoon—A violent tropical cyclone that occurs in the western Pacific or Indian oceans.

warlord—A military strongman.

BIBLIOGRAPHY

Arlidge, John. "Doha Unveils Its Secret Weapon, but Will It Work?" *The London Times*, November 29, 2008.

Barboza, David. "I.M. Pei in China, Revisiting Roots." *The New York Times*, October 9, 2006. Available online. URL: http://www.nytimes.com/2006/10/09/arts/design/09pei.html.

Boehm, Gero von. *Conversations with I.M. Pei: Light Is the Key*. New York: Prestel, 2000.

Campbell, Robert. "Rolling Out Rock's Monument: The Hall of Fame and Museum Will Be the 1990s' Most Hyped Architecture." *The Boston Globe*, August 27, 1995.

Cannell, Michael. *I.M. Pei: Mandarin of Modernism*. New York: Carol Southern Books, 1995.

Deitz, Paula. "Stones, Scrolls, and Scholars: I.M. Pei Makes a Poignant Return to His Native Suzhou." *The Architectural Review* 222 (October 2007), pp. 64–73.

Dupré, Judith. *Skyscrapers*. New York: Black Dog & Leventhal, 1996.

Hales, Linda. "Architect at the Apex; I.M. Pei's Pyramids and Sharp Angles Have Taken Him in One Direction: To the Top." *The Washington Post*, October 5, 2003.

Ivy, Robert. "At the Twilight of His Career, I.M. Pei Shows Few Signs of Slowing Down." *Architectural Record* 192 (June 2004): pp. 204–212.

———. "I.M. Pei Returns to His Family's Hometown in China and Designs the Suzhou Museum for a Sensitive, Historic Site." *Architectural Record* 195 (May 2007): pp. 186–191.

Jodidio, Philip, and Janet Adams Strong. *I.M. Pei: Complete Works*. New York: Rizzoli, 2008.

Ouroussoff, Nicolai. "For I.M. Pei, History Is Still Happening." *The New York Times*, December 12, 2008.

Santos, Carlos. "Globe-Trotting U.S. Citizens," *Richmond Times Dispatch*, July 5, 2005.

Wiseman, Carter. *I.M. Pei: A Profile in American Architecture.* Rev. ed. New York: Harry N. Abrams, 2001.
Yoshida, Kenji and Kei Yokoyama, eds. *I.M. Pei: Words for the Future.* Tokyo: A & U Publishing, 2008.

FURTHER RESOURCES

BOOKS

Englar, Mary. *I.M. Pei*. Chicago: Raintree, 2006.

Glancey, Jonathan. *The Story of Architecture*. London: DK, 2003.

Jodidio, Philip. *Museum of Islamic Art: Doha, Qatar*. New York: Prestel, 2009.

Khan, Hasan-Uddin. *International Style: Modernist Architecture from 1925 to 1965*. Los Angeles: Taschen, 2009.

Lashnits, Tom. *Maya Lin*. New York: Chelsea House, 2007.

Reid, Aileen. *I.M. Pei*. New York: Knickerbocker Press, 1998.

FILMS

Rosen, Peter. *First Person Singular: I.M. Pei/The Museum on the Mountain*. Digital Videodisc. New York: Peter Rosen Productions, 1997–1998.

WEB SITES

Great Buildings: I.M. Pei
http://www.greatbuildings.com/architects/I._M._Pei.html

Ieoh Ming Pei
http://www.worldofbiography.com/9172-I%20M%20Pei/life.asp

Pei, Cobb, Freed & Partners
http://www.pcfandp.com

The Pritzker Architecture Prize: I.M. Pei, 1983 Laureate
http://www.pritzkerprize.com/laureates/1983/index.html

PHOTO CREDITS

INDEX

ABOUT THE AUTHOR

LOUISE CHIPLEY SLAVICEK received her master's degree in history from the University of Connecticut. She is the author of numerous articles on American and world history for scholarly journals and young people's magazines, including *Cobblestone* and *Calliope*. Her more than two dozen books for young people include *Women of the American Revolution, Israel, The Great Wall of China*, and *Daniel Inouye*. She lives in Ohio with her husband, Jim, a research biologist, and their two children, Krista and Nathan.